Seals, Sea Lions and Sea Otters

ALASKA GEOGRAPHIC®, Volume 27, Number 2 / 2000

EDITOR
Penny Rennick

PRODUCTION DIRECTOR
Kathy Doogan

ASSOCIATE EDITOR
Susan Beeman

MARKETING DIRECTOR
Jill S. Brubaker

ADMINISTRATIVE ASSISTANT
Melanie Britton

ISBN: 1-56661-052-4

PRICE TO NON-MEMBERS THIS ISSUE: $21.95

PRINTED IN U.S.A.

POSTMASTER:
Send address changes to:
ALASKA GEOGRAPHIC®
P.O. Box 93370
Anchorage, Alaska 99509-3370

COVER: *Sea otters are the largest member of the weasel family Mustelidae, but the smallest marine mammal. They spend hours each day grooming their thick fur, which insulates them from the cold. (Patrick J. Endres)*

PREVIOUS PAGE: *Alaska is home to several Steller sea lion rookeries, where sea lions haul out to bear their young and mate. Pups and females surround a bull on Lowrie Island in Southeast, near the Canadian border. Steller sea lions were added to the endangered species list in 1990. (John Hyde)*

FACING PAGE: *Northern fur seals from the Pribilof Islands in the Bering Sea became the focus of commercial hunting from the late 1700s to early 1900s. Alaska Natives still kill some young bulls today for subsistence uses. (Roy Corral)*

ALASKA GEOGRAPHIC® (ISSN 0361-1353) is published quarterly by The Alaska Geographic Society, 639 West International Airport Rd. #38, Anchorage, AK 99518. Periodicals postage paid at Anchorage, Alaska, and additional mailing offices. Copyright © 2000 The Alaska Geographic Society. All rights reserved. Registered trademark: Alaska Geographic, ISSN 0361-1353; key title Alaska Geographic. This issue published June 2000.

THE ALASKA GEOGRAPHIC SOCIETY is a non-profit, educational organization dedicated to improving geographic understanding of Alaska and the North, putting geography back in the classroom and exploring new methods of teaching and learning.

MEMBERS RECEIVE *ALASKA GEOGRAPHIC®*, a high-quality, colorful quarterly that devotes each issue to monographic, in-depth coverage of a specific northern region or resource-oriented subject. Back issues are also available (see p. 96). Membership is $49 ($59 to non-U.S. addresses) per year. To order or to request a free catalog of back issues, contact: Alaska Geographic Society, P.O. Box 93370, Anchorage, AK 99509-3370; phone (907) 562-0164 or toll free (888) 255-6697, fax (907) 562-0479, e-mail: akgeo@akgeo.com. A complete listing of our back issues, maps and other products can also be found on our website at www.akgeo.com.

SUBMITTING PHOTOGRAPHS: Those interested in submitting photos for possible publication should write for a list of upcoming topics or other photo needs and a copy of our editorial guidelines. We cannot be responsible for unsolicited submissions. Please note that any submission not accompanied by sufficient postage for return by certified mail will be returned by regular mail.

CHANGE OF ADDRESS: When you move, the post office <u>may not automatically forward</u> your *ALASKA GEOGRAPHIC®*. To ensure continuous service, please notify us <u>at least six weeks</u> before moving. Send your new address and membership number or a mailing label from a recent issue of *ALASKA GEOGRAPHIC®* to: Address Change, Alaska Geographic Society, Box 93370, Anchorage, AK 99509-3370.

If your issue is returned to us by the post office because it is undeliverable, we will contact you to ask if you wish to receive a replacement for a small fee to cover the cost of additional postage to reship the issue.

SEPARATIONS: Graphic Chromatics

PRINTING: Banta Publications Group / Hart Press

ABOUT THIS ISSUE

Written by noted marine mammal experts, this issue explores in depth the seals, sea lions and sea otters that enhance Alaska's vibrant off-shore environment. *ALASKA GEOGRAPHIC®* focuses on these species because the state's marine waters are in flux. Precipitous population declines for Steller sea lions, and similar though less drastic declines for northern fur seals have prompted government officials to activate provisions of the Endangered Species Act. These actions affect commercial fisheries, tourism and other aspects of the state's economy and lifestyle.

We thank many researchers for help in gathering information and photos. In particular we appreciate the efforts of Mina Jacobs of the Anchorage Museum of History and Art; Steve Henrikson, collections curator at the Alaska State Museum in Juneau; Alice Ryser of the Baranof Museum in Kodiak; Jo Antonson, Alaska state historian; Bruce Merrill of the Z.J. Loussac Library, Anchorage; and Nancy Tileston of Alaska Resources Library and Information Services, Anchorage.

Bob Juettner of Aleutians East Borough pointed us to the marketing of canned sea lion meat in Japan. Finally, we thank the staffs of the Department of Interior's U.S. Fish and Wildlife Service and the Department of Commerce's National Oceanic and Atmospheric Administration for their help with innumerable questions. ■

The Library of Congress has cataloged this serial publication as follows:

Alaska Geographic. v.1-
[Anchorage, Alaska Geographic Society] 1972-
v. ill. (part col.). 23 x 31 cm.
Quarterly
Official publication of The Alaska Geographic Society.
Key title: Alaska geographic, ISSN 0361-1353.

1. Alaska—Description and travel—1959-
—Periodicals. I. Alaska Geographic Society.

F901.A266 917.98'04'505 72-92087

Library of Congress 75[79112] MARC-S.

Contents

Introduction

By Penny Rennick and Susan Beeman

As the boat cruised Icy Strait near Glacier Bay in Southeast Alaska, a life-and-death drama played out off its port and starboard sides. A pod of killer whales cut the water off its port side, while a herd of Steller sea lions hugged the rocky shore off its starboard, swimming in the opposite direction and hoping to avoid the whales' teeth-filled jaws. This act could occur in many locations along Alaska's lengthy coastline. The North Pacific and Bering, Chukchi and Beaufort seas shelter a variety of marine mammals, including seals, sea lions and sea otters. Alaskans and visitors have observed these animals from onshore for centuries, but once the animals dive beneath the ocean's waves, they enter a world hidden from an

observer's view. Questions about their undersea life have always intrigued people. Does a harbor seal spend its whole life in one area? What route do fur seals take during migration? Why is the Steller sea lion population continuing to decline? Do sea otters really use rocks as tools?

Biologists research these questions and many more. Marine mammals are less visible than their terrestrial cousins, and more difficult to track. New technologies, however, are providing easier, more efficient means of learning, for example, how deep a seal dives, and for how long it remains under water; a seal blubber analysis reveals what the animal has been eating; and information about weather patterns such as El Niño guide

scientists in their understanding of how water temperature affects the foods that Steller sea lions consume. Simple observation teaches researchers about the daily lives of these animals: how much they sleep, what time of year they mate, how often throughout the day a pup nurses.

Marine mammal biologists come together in these pages to discuss Alaska's five main seal species (harbor,

FACING PAGE: *Researchers at the White Sisters rookery observe Steller sea lions in the fog. Biologists have been studying why the sea lion population has declined in recent years. (John Hyde)*

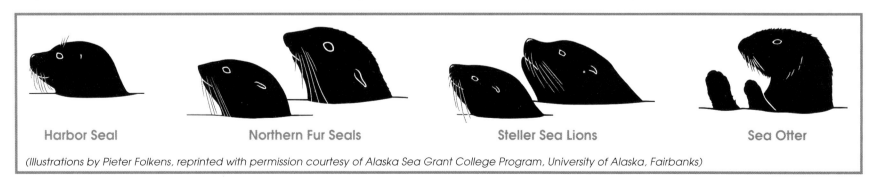

Harbor Seal   Northern Fur Seals   Steller Sea Lions   Sea Otter

(Illustrations by Pieter Folkens, reprinted with permission courtesy of Alaska Sea Grant College Program, University of Alaska, Fairbanks)

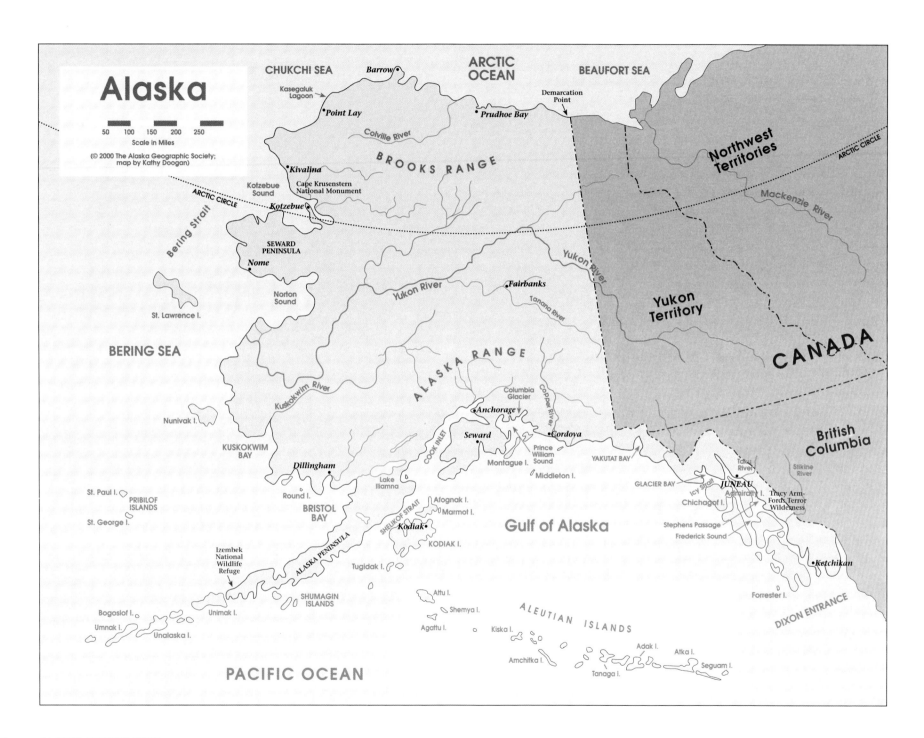

Alaska

50 100 150 200 250
Scale in Miles

(© 2000 The Alaska Geographic Society;
map by Kathy Doogan)

CHUKCHI SEA

ARCTIC OCEAN

BEAUFORT SEA

Barrow

Kasegaluk Lagoon

Point Lay

Demarcation Point

Prudhoe Bay

Colville River

BROOKS RANGE

Northwest Territories

ARCTIC CIRCLE

Kivalina

Cape Krusenstern National Monument

Kotzebue Sound

Mackenzie River

ARCTIC CIRCLE

Kotzebue

Bering Strait

SEWARD PENINSULA

Nome

Yukon River

Yukon River

Yukon Territory

St. Lawrence I.

Norton Sound

Fairbanks

Tanana River

BERING SEA

ALASKA RANGE

CANADA

Kuskokwim River

Columbia Glacier

Copper River

Nunivak I.

Anchorage

Seward

Cordova

British Columbia

KUSKOKWIM BAY

Prince William Sound

Montague I.

YAKUTAT BAY

Taku River

Stikine River

Dillingham

Lake Iliamna

Middleton I.

GLACIER BAY

Icy Strait

JUNEAU

Admiralty I.

Tracy Arm-Fords Terror Wilderness

St. Paul I.

PRIBILOF ISLANDS

Round I.

BRISTOL BAY

Afognak I.

Marmot I.

Gulf of Alaska

Chichagof I.

St. George I.

SHELIKOF STRAIT

Kodiak

KODIAK I.

Stephens Passage

Frederick Sound

Izembek National Wildlife Refuge

ALASKA PENINSULA

Tugidak I.

Ketchikan

Bogoslof I.

SHUMAGIN ISLANDS

Attu I.

Forrester I.

Umnak I.

Unimak I.

Shemya I.

ALEUTIAN ISLANDS

DIXON ENTRANCE

Unalaska I.

Agattu I.

Kiska I.

Adak I.

Atka I.

Seguam I.

PACIFIC OCEAN

Amchitka I.

Tanaga I.

Distinct markings of the ribbon seal make identification of Phoca fasciata *easy. The pelage of other seal species that inhabit Alaska waters aren't so unique, and they are more difficult to distinguish. (Kathy Frost, ADFG)*

Taxonomic Classification for Alaska seals, northern fur seals, Steller sea lions and sea otters

CLASS	ORDER	SUBORDER	FAMILY	GENUS AND SPECIES
Mammalia				
	Carnivora			
		Pinnipedia (fin-footed)		
			Phocidae (earless seals)	
				Phoca vitulina (harbor seal)
				Phoca largha (spotted seal)
				Phoca fasciata (ribbon seal)
				Phoca hispida (ringed seal)
				Erignathus barbatus (bearded seal)
				Mirounga angustirostris (n. elephant seal)
				Cystophora cristata (hooded seal)
			Otariidae (eared seals)	
				Callorhinus ursinus (northern fur seal)
				Eumetopias jubatus (Steller sea lion)
		Fissipedia (split-footed)		
			Mustelidae	
				Enhydra lutris (sea otter)

(Compiled from *Marine Mammals of Eastern North Pacific and Arctic Waters.* Edited by Delphine Haley. Second Edition, Revised. Seattle: Pacific Search Press, 1986; and *Guide to Marine Mammals of Alaska.* By Kate Wynne. Illustrated by Pieter Folkens. Fairbanks: Alaska Sea Grant College Program, University of Alaska Fairbanks, 1992.)

spotted, ribbon, bearded and ringed), northern fur seals, Steller sea lions and sea otters. Their expertise adds depth and clarity to the complexities of these animals' lives.

Seals, fur seals, sea lions and sea otters all belong to the same order Carnivora under the class Mammalia. Confusion often arises over the classification of the fur seal. They are not "true seals," as they have visible ears like the sea lion and in fact belong to the same family. Fur seals are placed here in a separate chapter. The species of seals covered in this issue are in the family Phocidae (earless seals), while northern fur seals and Steller sea lions belong to the family Otariidae (eared seals) having visible, inch-long, furled ears. Sea otters are members of the Mustelidae family. Scientists further classify the seals, northern fur seal and Steller sea lion as the suborder Pinnipedia, meaning "fin-footed," while the sea otter belongs to the suborder Fissipedia, or "split-footed." Though the three families look different from each other, and possess different aquatic adaptations, they are related.

Biologists think marine mammals evolved from terrestrial ancestors through a series of adaptations to life in the sea. Marine mammals live in all the oceans of the world. Some eat only plants; some eat other animals. Like land mammals, marine mammals breathe air through lungs, are warm-blooded, bear live offspring and suckle their young. For hydration, most marine mammals rely on water in their food rather than drinking fresh water; they produce urine that is saltier than the sea.

Read along as *ALASKA GEOGRAPHIC*® takes a closer look at Alaska's seals, sea lions and sea otters. ■

Seals

By Lloyd Lowry and Kathy Frost

EDITOR'S NOTE: *The husband and wife team of Lloyd Lowry and Kathy Frost, both Alaska Department of Fish and Game biologists, have been studying marine mammals since 1975 in all parts of Alaska, focusing on nutrition, natural history and ecology. Lowry was Marine Mammals Coordinator for ADFG from 1986 to June 2000, when he retired from state work. He is chairman of the U.S. Marine Mammal Commission's Committee of Scientific Advisors and the Steller Sea Lion Recovery Team.*

The first time we went in the field in Alaska to study ice seals we were doing spring work at the ice edge, catching and tagging pups, doing surveys. This was the first time Kathy had seen sea ice, and the first time she'd seen ice seals. We were based on the NOAA ship *Surveyor* and using a helicopter to catch and tag seal pups.

Lloyd had gone to sea a month earlier, so was the "expert." We went by helicopter to tag Kathy's first seal pup, a female spotted seal with a small pup, on the ice floe. As we started to land, Kathy asked Lloyd, "What about the mothers? What do they do and what do we do?" He replied, "You don't have to worry about them, they always jump in the water before you ever get to the pup." The helicopter set down; we jumped out the door and raced to catch the pup, only to be met by a ferocious-looking mother seal who was firmly standing her ground, protecting her pup with teeth bared. No matter what we tried, we never did get to tag that pup. So much for mother seals never defending their pups. To our recollection, that was the only time in the ensuing 25 years that ever happened, but it was quite an introduction to working with seals on sea ice.

The coastlines and seas of Alaska are home to a great number of seals. Seals can be seen nearly everywhere, from the rocky fiords of Southeast Alaska where harbor seals abound to the permanent arctic ice pack where ringed and bearded seals live. The sheer size of the area and the richness and diversity of marine habitats allow several very different species to flourish.

There are five species of seals that are truly Alaska residents, and they will each be discussed in detail in this chapter. Two others occur often enough to merit brief mention: the northern elephant seal and the hooded seal. The huge northern elephant seal (*Mirounga angustirostris*) was thought to have been hunted to extinction by 1892, but has bounced back remarkably and is now numerous on its rookeries along the coast of California and Mexico. Over the years, elephant seals, alive and dead, have occasionally been reported in Southeast Alaska, the Gulf of Alaska and the Aleutian Islands. These observations were generally considered "extralimital occurrences" — sightings of animals that had wandered far outside their normal range. However, when researchers began putting instruments

FACING PAGE: *A Pacific harbor seal,* Phoca vitulina richardsi, *rests on ice in Endicott Arm in Southeast. In Alaska, harbor seals range from Kuskokwim Bay south along the coast to Southeast, and westward to the Aleutian and Pribilof islands. (Tom Walker)*

Only rarely seen in Alaska, hooded seals do occasionally stray from the North Atlantic and have been sighted from Prudhoe Bay, on the arctic coast, to Bering Strait, near the Seward Peninsula. They have even been seen as far south as Florida and Portugal. (Fred Bruemmer)

on elephant seals to track their movements at sea, the results were surprising. It turns out that when individuals, especially males, leave their rookeries for their post-breeding (February-June) and post-molting (July-December) feeding trips, they commonly travel to deep-water areas off the coast of

southern Alaska. So, the sightings of elephant seals in Alaska are not all that unusual, and may become increasingly common as their population continues to grow.

The hooded seal comes to Alaska from a different direction, the east. This species (*Cystophora cristata*) occurs in the pack ice of the central and western North Atlantic and occasionally makes it to Alaska. Hooded seals were reported three times in the Prudhoe Bay region from 1970 to 1975. One instance was particularly interesting because the seal appeared in a hole drilled in the Kuparuk River ice in mid-December. It

was captured after it climbed out of the hole and began wandering across the tundra, and was given an airplane ride to the University of Alaska in Fairbanks. Hooded seals are known to be particularly aggressive, and this one earned the nickname "Jaws" after it decided to bite Dr. Bud Fay when he went into its cage. We don't know how frequently hooded seals reach Alaska, but Eskimo lore suggests that in the past they have made it as far as Bering Strait.

What makes a seal?

Seals are truly amphibious animals, alternating periods hauled out on land or ice with trips to sea to feed. They probably evolved from an otterlike ancestor about 20 million years ago. They are warm-blooded, air-breathing marine mammals that nurse their young.

While they are a diverse group showing specialized adaptations to the places they live, northern seals have a number of traits in common. They're basically shaped like an elongate watermelon, with a relative small head, short front flippers and hind flippers that extend straight behind the body. A seal's muscle and skeleton is wrapped in a thick blanket of blubber that makes up 25 to 50 percent or more of its total body weight. The blubber streamlines the body, insulates it against cold air and water, and provides an energy reserve. The thickness of blubber and therefore the fatness of seals vary seasonally with changes in food availability and feeding activity.

Seals older than pups have a relatively sparse coat of short hair. The coat is molted once a year, sometime between late spring and early fall. During the molt, seals come ashore often and bask in the sunshine, which keeps them warm and promotes growth of the skin and hair. They feed less during the molt, and lose weight.

Seals are long-lived animals. Average life spans are around 20 years; some may live to be 40 or more. They grow fairly rapidly for the first 10 years or so, then growth slows. Both males and females become sexually active at 3 to 7 years old. Adult females usually produce a single pup each spring that is nursed for a few weeks, then abruptly weaned when the mother leaves. Breeding occurs in late spring or early summer, after pups are weaned.

Seals go into the water to feed, and they are obviously good swimmers and divers. They have a number of physiological and anatomical adaptations that allow them to stay submerged for 20 minutes or more. When they are at sea feeding, they may spend as much as 90 percent of the time underwater.

A harbor seal is restrained for testing by biologists in Prince William Sound. Harbor seals are difficult to count, as only a portion of the total number in a given area is hauled out at one time. (Roy Corral)

Pacific Harbor Seal

Introduction

When most people in mainstream America talk about seals, they are usually referring to harbor seals. These common animals occur along the east and west coasts of North America, and because they are so widespread and so easy to maintain in captivity, harbor seals are found in zoos and aquariums around the world. The widely known and popular "talking" seal Andre was a harbor seal from Camden, Maine. Harbor seals are not, however, the same as the "seals" seen in circus acts. Those ball-balancing performers are, in fact, not seals at all. They are sea lions. Harbor seals — with their fat, sausage-like bodies and short, straight hind flippers — are poorly suited to such games.

The scientific name for Pacific harbor seals is *Phoca vitulina richardsi*. They belong to the family Phocidae, which includes other earless seals in Alaska such as ringed, ribbon, bearded and spotted seals. Harbor seals are often called hair seals by coastal residents of southern Alaska. In many parts of the world, they are called common seals.

Description — Size, Coloration, Senses, Vocalizations

Harbor seals are medium-sized earless seals. They are covered with short, stiff hair; their coloration varies, but follows two basic patterns. The coats of dark phase seals have a gray background with light rings and light and dark blotches or spots. Light phase seals have light sides and belly with dark blotches or spots. Once each year, harbor seals molt, or shed their old hair, and grow a new coat. During this molting period, seals spend more time hauled out than they do at other times, probably because the new hair grows faster when the seals are out of water and the skin is warmer. While seals are molting, their metabolism drops almost 20 percent. This slower metabolism lowers their food requirements and allows them to spend long hours hauled out instead of feeding. Data from tagged seals indicates that seals may spend 60 percent or more of their time hauled out during the molt, compared to less than 20 percent in winter. The shedding of hair takes four to six weeks and occurs at different times for seals of different ages and sex, but usually occurs in mid- to late summer, after pupping. Yearlings, which didn't molt as pups, usually molt first,

Above water, harbor seals move like inchworms. They cannot rotate their hind flippers forward for locomotion or lift their belly from the ground when on land or ice. (Gary Schultz)

followed by adult females, subadults and lastly the males. Seals often appear dull and yellow-brown before the molt. Afterwards they sport bright, shiny new coats.

In Alaska, harbor seal pups weigh about 24 pounds at birth and gain weight rapidly during a month-long nursing period. They may more than double their weight during this time. The largest weaned pup captured in recent years in Prince William Sound weighed more than 70 pounds. The average weight for adults is 165 to 185 pounds; males are somewhat larger than females.

Harbor seals can see both above and below the water. Their eyes are adapted to see well at low light levels, such as at night or in deep water where not much light penetrates. They also have good hearing, which is directional both above and below water. Their hearing in air works the same as hearing in other land mammals; however, they have special modifications to the inner ear that make directional hearing underwater possible. They have a good sense of smell above water, which allows them to distinguish their pups from other pups on a haulout. Harbor seals vocalize, just like many other mammals. Adults bark; young pups (before they are weaned) have a characteristic bawl when they are separated from their mothers. In fact, when biologists have a hard time distinguishing very big pups from small yearlings, the voice tells the tale.

Bald eagles take advantage of blood and after-birth left on the ice from a harbor seal birth in Tracy Arm-Fords Terror Wilderness, in Southeast's Tongass National Forest. (John Hyde)

Distribution, Migration, Population Status

Harbor seals occur in both the North Atlantic and North Pacific oceans. The subspecies found in Alaska, *P. v. richardsi*, occurs widely in the eastern North Pacific, from Baja, California to Bristol Bay, Alaska. They are also found all along the Aleutian Islands.

Harbor seals are usually found in near-shore coastal waters where they feed, haul out to rest, give birth, care for their young and molt. Hauling-out areas include intertidal reefs, rocky shores, mud- and sandbars, floating glacial ice, and gravel and sand beaches. Harbor seals are sometimes found in rivers and lakes, usually on a seasonal basis, present in summer, absent in winter. In Lake Iliamna, seals are present year-round and are almost certainly resident. Although most harbor seals are associated closely with coastal waters, they are also found on Middleton Island in the northern Gulf of Alaska, more than 50 miles from the mainland, and on the Pribilof Islands in the central Bering Sea.

Harbor seals tend to use haulout sites where they have protection from predators, direct access to deep water, proximity to food and protection from strong winds and high surf. Based on satellite-tagging studies in Alaska, most adult harbor seals use the same few haulout sites all year. During spring and summer in Prince William Sound, each tagged seal used an average of four different haulouts, while in fall and winter they used an average of only two. More than half the time, they used one preferred site.

The distribution and movements of harbor seals at sea are not as well understood as their hauling-out behavior. Recently, however, considerable information about at-sea behavior has become available through

Satellite Tagging

By Kathy Frost

Seals have always been hard to study because they spend so much of their time in and under the water where biologists can't see them. For this reason, more has always been known about their behavior on land — where they usually spend less than 40 percent of their time — than in the water where they feed and make their living. In the last 10 years, however, a new technique has been developed that gives biologists a window into the secret lives of seals when they are under water.

This new tool is satellite tags. These

Researchers Kathy Frost (left) and Gay Sheffield glue a satellite tagging device onto a harbor seal's back. When the seal molts, the device falls off. (Roy Corral)

small transmitters — about the size of a small cell phone and powered by batteries — send data to earth-orbiting satellites telling what the seal is doing 24 hours a day. Not only is it possible to know where the seal is, but small on-board computers also collect information about how deep and how long the seals dive. Biologists can sit at office computers and know what seals are doing hundreds of miles away in the open ocean of the Gulf of Alaska or the pack ice of the Bering Sea.

Although satellite tags are incredibly sophisticated instruments, the method for attaching them is simple. They are glued to the seal's fur using a quick-setting five-minute epoxy. This has several advantages — it is quick and easy to do in the field, and it doesn't last forever. When tagged seals shed their fur during the annual molt, the satellite tag falls off — ensuring that the seals won't have to carry the tag for life. Satellite tags are expensive — more than $4,000 each plus another $2,000 to retrieve the data – but they save hundreds of hours of flying and provide insights into seal movements and behavior that biologists can get no other way.

In Alaska, satellite tags have been attached to harbor seals, spotted seals and ringed seals. Knowledge of these seals has grown by leaps and bounds — even from only a few tags. As these tags get smaller and more sophisticated in the future, biologists will learn more and more about the secret lives of Alaska's seals. ■

the use of satellite-linked tags. These tags allow scientists to track seals and monitor their diving behavior when they are in the water and far from land.

Unlike many other species of marine mammals, harbor seals do not make long annual migrations. Most tagged harbor seals stay within about 20 miles of their haulouts throughout the time they are tagged. A few seals, mostly young animals, have made substantial movements away from their tagging locations. One subadult tagged at Channel Island in Prince William Sound swam more than 200 miles to Yakutat Bay where it spent the winter making repeated trips offshore into the Gulf of Alaska. A pup tagged in the Sound traveled more than 200 miles to Cook Inlet where it remained throughout the winter. Several others made regular feeding trips to Middleton Island, the Gulf of Alaska or the Copper River Delta.

In northern Bristol Bay, harbor seals may "migrate" in cold years when sea ice covers their habitat along the coast. To reach ice-free waters, these seals would have to swim several hundreds of miles. Such hypothesized migrations have not yet been documented, but scientists hope satellite-tagging studies someday will do so. Biologists do not yet know how harbor seals find their way back to their traditional haulouts in years when they have to make these lengthy swims.

Harbor seals are difficult to census because they can be accurately counted only when they are hauled out. They haul out in hundreds of locations in Alaska, and even if seals at all sites could be counted, not all the seals haul out at the same time. For this reason, the exact number of harbor seals in Alaska is unknown. The most recent (1990s) population estimate by the National Marine Mammal Laboratory is 78,500 for the whole state.

Because harbor seals use haulouts spread all along the coast, biologists often keep track of their populations by monitoring certain areas called trend count areas. Currently, there are trend count areas in Southeast Alaska (Sitka and Ketchikan), the northern Gulf of Alaska (Tugidak Island, Kodiak Archipelago and Prince William Sound) and Bristol Bay. Population trends are not the same in all areas. In general, seal populations in Southeast Alaska are stable or increasing. However, in the northern Gulf of Alaska, there has been a major population decline since the 1970s. At Tugidak Island, south of Kodiak, the average counts declined by 85 percent from 1976 to 1988. Recently the decline at Tugidak appears to have leveled off. In Prince William Sound, the number of seals at 25 indicator sites declined by more than 50 percent from 1984 to 1999. Reasons for these declines are unknown and are the subject of ongoing studies by the Alaska Department of Fish and Game (ADFG), the National Marine Fisheries Service (NMFS) and the University of Alaska.

Biologists suspect that a period of ocean warming in the late 1970s dramatically changed the abundance of forage fishes and invertebrates, and made food less available to harbor seals, especially pups and juveniles.

BELOW: *Harbor seal pups are born with their eyes open and have a short coat like that of adults. They are able to crawl and swim immediately. (John Hyde)*

RIGHT: *Biologists release a harbor seal back into the water after gathering research data near Applegate Rock, in Prince William Sound. (Roy Corral)*

FACING PAGE: *In the 1970s, thousands of harbor seals hauled out on a sandbar in the Moffett Point-Strawberry Point area of Izembek Lagoon within Izembek National Wildlife Refuge near the tip of the Alaska Peninsula.* (John Sarvis)

Diet, Feeding Habits

Most information about the diet of harbor seals in Alaska was collected more than 20 years ago in the mid-1970s. The most common prey in the stomachs of seals examined in both Prince William Sound and the northern Gulf of Alaska included walleye pollock, Pacific cod, capelin, eulachon, Pacific herring, salmon, octopus and squid. Pollock was eaten most often, but even so, more than 50 percent of the

Fatty Acids

By Kathy Frost

When I was little, I remember my grandmother telling me to eat my vegetables and other things that were good for me. "You are what you eat," she would tell me. Years later, when I first moved to Alaska, I remember my Eskimo friends telling me that bearded seals were good to eat "because they ate things that tasted good — like clams and shrimp," and that spotted seals weren't so good because they tasted like the fish they ate. At the time, many people considered these just old wives' tales.

Now, many years later, biologists have uncovered the scientific explanation for why both my grandmother and my Eskimo friends were right: fatty acids. Fatty acids are the building blocks of fat. It turns out that when an animal like a seal eats something, the fatty acids in the prey are transferred intact and unaltered into the seal's blubber — a good reason for the seal to taste like what it eats.

The "fatty acid signature" of every prey species is distinct because there are more than 70 different types of fatty acids, and each different kind of fish or invertebrate has a different mix of fatty acids. Even within different age groups or geographic regions, the fatty acids may be distinct. For this reason, it is possible to analyze the blubber of a seal using a technique called "fatty acids signature analysis" and know what it ate by using a chemical matching technique. This procedure doesn't give the details of every meal, but an estimate of what foods were important in the seal's overall energy budget.

By using fatty acids analysis, biologists now know there are substantial regional differences in what seals eat. They don't all go to some central feeding ground and eat the same thing. The diets of seals from haulouts only a few miles apart differ substantially. For example, seals living in Port Chalmers in southern Prince William Sound eat lots of flatfish, which are abundant in this shallow region. In spring, when herring arrive to spawn along the shores of Montague Island, harbor seals eat lots of these egg-filled, high-fat fish. When hooligan (smelt) runs begin in the Copper River Delta, many harbor seals move to this area to take advantage of this seasonally abundant food resource. The fatty acid signature of each of these species is different, allowing biologists to document these changes in diet by season and area. ▪

The foods a seal eats determine its "fatty acid signature." Biologists use blubber analysis to learn what seals are consuming. Here, a young elephant seal, or "weaner," chews on seaweed. (Frank S. Balthis)

stomachs contained prey items other than pollock. Young seals ate a lot of capelin, eulachon and herring, species high in fat and a good energy source for young, fast-growing seals.

More recently, biologists are using new tools to study harbor seal diets. One of those is fatty acid signature analysis. By examining the fatty acid composition of a small piece of blubber, it is possible to estimate what made up the seal's diet during the last few months. Fatty acids analysis indicates that seals in the 1990s were eating more flatfish than they did 20 years ago, and that overall, their diets are less diverse.

Breeding, Young

Harbor seal females give birth to a single pup once a year, usually on land or on glacial ice. In Alaska, harbor seal pups are born between mid-May and mid-July in the same general locations that are used as haulouts at other times of the year. However, pregnant females usually move to isolated sites or to the edge of large groups to give birth and remain there while the pups are very young. Later the females with pups return to the main haulout area.

Harbor seal pups are born with their eyes open and with an adultlike coat. They are able to swim almost immed-iately after birth, and remain close to their mothers even when they are in the water. This is unlike some other seal or sea lion species, where the pups remain on the ice or land while the mother goes to sea to feed. Harbor seal pups normally nurse for about one month by which time they may consist of more than 40 percent fat. This fat provides an

LEFT: *A harbor seal rests on kelp-covered rocks in Dangerous Passage, in western Prince William Sound. Harbor seals have adapted to a wide variety of terrestrial environments. (Alissa Crandall)*

BELOW: *Using its hind flippers for propulsion and front flippers to help steer, a harbor seal is at ease in water. This species eats a range of marine creatures, including herring, flounder, salmon, eulachon, cod, rockfish, sculpin, sand lance, octopus, squid and shrimp. (George Matz)*

energy reserve to tide the pup over while it is learning to feed on its own.

Adult females breed about two weeks after their pups are weaned. Harbor seals become sexually mature between ages 3 and 7. Exactly when they mature within this four-year range depends to a great degree on environmental conditions. When food resources are scarce and/or seals are close to the carrying capacity of their habitat, maturity is delayed. When resources are abundant, young seals grow quickly and mature at an earlier age. The sex ratio of harbor seals at birth is approximately equal and remains so until about 5 years of age. After that, mortality rates for males are higher, and females become relatively more abundant. The maximum ages of harbor seals, based on growth layers in their teeth, are 26 years for a male and 32 years for a female.

Predation, Hunting

Harbor seals are one of the top predators in the marine ecosystems of Alaska. They eat many of the same prey (e.g. pollock, herring, capelin) that are also eaten by seabirds, fishes and other marine mammals. In addition, harbor seals become food for other species including killer whales, Steller sea lions and sharks.

The impact of predators on harbor seal populations is unknown, but may be significant. In some areas, harbor seals make up about 25 percent of the diet of killer whales. In Prince William

Sex ratios between males and females are about equal for harbor seal pups such as this one inching its way along a beach. (Frank S. Balthis)

Sound alone, killer whales may eat up to 400 harbor seals per year. The incidence of sharks caught on halibut longlines in the Gulf of Alaska has increased greatly in the last decade. Biologists don't know how many seals these sharks may eat, but seals have been found in their stomachs. In other areas like Hawaii and Sable Island, Nova Scotia, sharks kill a significant number of pups and young seals each year, and can have a substantial impact on survival.

Harbor seals were hunted commercially in Alaska from the late 1800s through 1972. For many years, seal harvests were encouraged to decrease conflicts with fisheries. However, since implementation of the Marine Mammal Protection Act in 1972, hunting of harbor seals has been restricted to Alaska Natives. Harbor seal meat is the "hamburger" of many small coastal communities and their skins are used in making Native handicrafts such as sealskin parkas, mittens and hats. For all of Alaska, the subsistence harvest of harbor seals is about 2,500 each year.

Adaptations to Environment

Unlike their terrestrial mammalian cousins, harbor seals are truly at home in the sea. They regularly dive and feed in water that is 150 to 500 feet deep. The deepest recorded dive for a harbor seal is 1,620 feet by an adult male seal in Southeast Alaska. Oxygen-conserving adaptations that allow such dives include reduced peripheral blood circulation, reduced heart rate and high levels of myoglobin (muscle oxygen binder). One-month-old harbor seal pups are already able to hold their breath and slow their heart rate to conserve oxygen.

Harbor seals are graceful, efficient swimmers as they use their hind flippers for propulsion and foreflippers as rudders. The blanket of blubber that surrounds them is not only an energy reserve, but also gives them a streamlined shape that is more efficient for swimming. Movement on land, however, is slow and awkward.

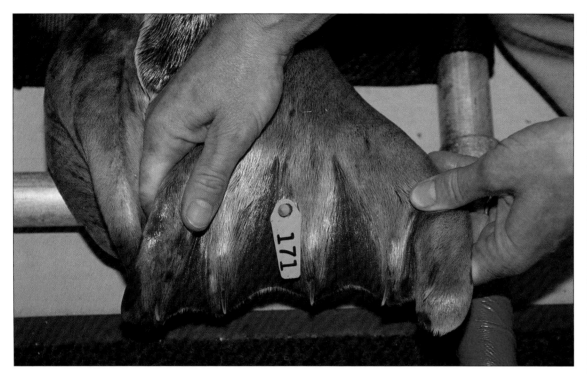

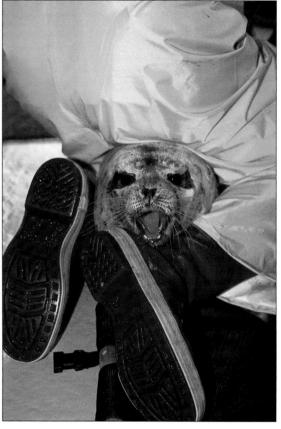

Research on the Species

In the last 10 years, there has been a lot of exciting research on harbor seals in Alaska. Some of those studies began because the 1989 *Exxon Valdez* oil spill impacted harbor seals in Prince William Sound. Other research in Southeast Alaska and near Kodiak is exploring why harbor seals have declined so dramatically since the 1970s. Since 1992, biologists in Alaska have attached satellite tags to more than 55 pups and 100 older seals to study their movements and diving behavior. A new technique for fatty acid signature analysis now allows biologists to use small blubber biopsies from the seals they catch during tagging to understand what seals are eating. They are also studying how different diets — such as herring and pollock — affect how fast seals grow and gain weight. Sophisticated computer software is being used to analyze photographs of seals to individually identify them — much the same way killer whales or humpback whales can be identified by the color patterns on their fins and flukes. Genetics studies are revealing how harbor seals from different regions are related to each other.

The field of harbor seal research is active and exciting. New insights from this research will help us better manage and conserve harbor seals for the future.

ABOVE LEFT: *Tagging allows biologists to track movements of individual harbor seals. This one was caught and tagged on Montague Island. (Roy Corral)*

ABOVE: *A harbor seal squawks as a biologist secures it for sampling and tagging. (Roy Corral)*

FACING PAGE: *Large groups of harbor seals, like this one hauled out on Channel Island in Prince William Sound, are common. These seals do not stray far from water and are wary of disturbances. (David Rhode)*

Spotted (Largha) Seal

Introduction

The taxonomy of the spotted seal has been the most controversial of any Alaska pinniped. Their close similarity in form and structure to the harbor seal and their overlapping distributions suggested that spotted seals should only be a subspecies of harbor seals. But the substantial differences in life history traits (described below) argued that while some interbreeding might occur it should be very slight. It was not until 1977 that detailed studies of distributions, coat patterns, measurements of bodies and skulls, and life histories led researchers to conclude that spotted seals deserved to be recognized as a full species, *Phoca largha*. Their conclusions, although somewhat tentative at the time, have turned out to be right, as recent molecular genetics studies have found distinct differences in the mitochondrial DNA of spotted seals and harbor seals.

Description — Size, Coloration, Senses, Vocalizations

Adult spotted seals look virtually identical to light phase harbor seals, with a silvery coat, darker on the back, and dark gray spots scattered over the body. They are about 5 feet long and weigh 150 to 250 pounds. Spotted seals are generally wary of people and seem to have unusually good hearing. When ADFG biologists began flying aerial surveys of spotted seals hauled out on sandbars in Kasegaluk Lagoon near Point Lay on the arctic coast, they approached the seals at an altitude of 1,000 feet as they usually do with other species. The spotted seals all immediately went into the water before the biologists got close enough to count. The scientists found that they had to approach the animals at an altitude of at least 3,000 feet to keep from spooking them into the water. The best explanation for this extraordinary response is that Alaska Natives hunt those seals, and the distant sound of the airplane probably resembles an outboard-powered skiff.

Spotted seal pups are very vocal, and squall frequently to get the attention of their mothers. Older seals in captivity made a variety of sounds both in air and underwater that have been described as "growls, chirps, barks, drums, and creaky doors." Functions of such sounds

Spotted, or largha, seals (Phoca largha) look nearly identical to harbor seals, but their habitat is much different. Spotted seals occur in areas of the North Pacific that are seasonally covered with sea ice. In Alaska, the Bering, Chukchi and Beaufort seas are home to this species. (Kathy Frost, ADFG)

Decorative mukluks, *made from bearded seal skin, keep feet warm and honor the subsistence tradition of Yup'ik Eskimos. (Steve McCutcheon Collection, Anchorage Museum of History and Art)*

are unknown, but they are made most frequently during the breeding season.

Distribution, Migration, Population Status

Spotted seals are widely distributed in the North Pacific, generally occurring in areas that are seasonally covered with sea ice. They range westward from Bristol Bay to Kamchatka in Russia, then south into the Sea of Japan. During summer they move northward into the Chukchi, Beaufort and East Siberian seas. From November through May or June they are found in the sea ice. In spring they are seen hauled out singly or in small groups, mostly in the ice front where the floes are not too congested and move freely. In summer and early fall spotted seals occur mostly in open water and may be seen hauled out in groups of 1,000 or more on sandy spits and bars along the coast. In the Chukchi Sea they make long trips to sea to feed, sometimes covering 500 miles or more. When we tracked them with satellite-linked tags, their speeds averaged about 3 mph when they were on feeding trips.

Alaska spotted seals occur seasonally over vast areas of the Bering, Chukchi, and Beaufort seas. The distance that they migrate depends largely on where they spend the summer months. Seals that summer in Kuskokwim Bay need to move only a short way from the sea ice where they spend winter and spring. In contrast, a spotted seal that summers in Kasegaluk Lagoon is 900 miles to the north of the usual location of the ice front.

Spotted seals are common off Alaska and their population may number 100,000 or more. However, there hasn't been a satisfactory method developed for estimating total population size. As is true for most seals, it is fairly easy to count them but much more difficult to know how many animals are being missed. Tagging studies suggest that during summer, spotted seals spend about 16 percent of their time near coastal haulouts. Therefore, at Kasegaluk Lagoon where biologists commonly counted 2,000 seals, the actual number of animals using the region may have been about 12,000.

Diet/Feeding Habits

Spotted seals feed on a wide variety of fishes and invertebrates. Shrimps and other crustaceans are especially important foods for young animals. Older animals still eat shrimps, but depend more on arctic cod, saffron cod, herring, capelin and other small- to medium-sized fishes. During summer

Spotted seal pups are born from late March to mid-April. Covered in lanugo, a white, woolly coat, they are protected from cold temperatures until they shed this two to four weeks later, revealing a coat similar to that of an adult. (Kathy Frost, ADFG)

along the coast of Kamchatka, spotted seals eat salmonids, mostly pink salmon. Biologists have not found salmon to be a major food in Alaska, but have never sampled the spotted seals that spend the summer in Kuskokwim Bay where such predation might occur. Fred DiCicco, a biologist who studies arctic charr, has seen scars from seal attacks on fishes in the Wulik River near Kivalina, north of Kotzebue. In one year when the charr run was later than usual, more than 20 percent of the fish he looked at had seal marks on them.

Breeding, Young

Spotted seal pups are born on the sea ice in March to April. They appear with a coat of long, white hair (lanugo), and weigh 15 to 20 pounds at birth.

They nurse for about four weeks, gain 30 to 40 pounds in weight, and then are weaned. At about the time of weaning they molt their lanugo and have an adultlike coat. The largest spotted seal pup Fairbanks ADFG biologists ever weighed was almost 80 pounds.

Spotted seals have an unusual breeding pattern. Sometime shortly after the pup is born, a male seal joins the mother-pup pair to form a triad. The male stays with the female until she ovulates some time after weaning and then they mate. Mating behavior has not been described in the wild, but captive seals copulated underwater.

Predation, Hunting

The ice-front zone where spotted seals spend winter and spring is generally to the south of polar bear territory, reducing the chances that they'll get eaten. However, biologists have recorded several instances where walrus have caught and eaten spotted seal pups. It seems that such interactions are more common in years with less than the usual amount of sea ice, which forces seals and walrus closer together. When hauling out along the coast, spotted seals may be exposed to predation by grizzly bears, but they tend to come ashore on low-lying bars with an unobstructed view and are probably rarely caught unaware. During their long summer feeding trips, they may run into killer whales.

Spotted seals are killed by Alaska Native subsistence hunters all along the west coast from Kuskokwim Bay to Barrow. Many are taken by villagers in the Bering Strait region during their spring and fall migrations. In summer they are hunted by villagers that are near their haulouts and feeding areas. The meat is a staple in the diet of coastal Eskimos, and the hides are used for making garments and other handicrafts. Soviet ship-based commercial hunters took a few thousand animals each year in the 1970s and 1980s, but their harvests of all species of ice-associated seals in the Bering and Chukchi seas have diminished to low levels since the breakup of the Soviet Union.

Research — Alaska Style

By Kathy Frost

Studying spotted seals in Point Lay is a lot different than studying seals in most parts of the United States. Alaska's Point Lay has no hotel, no roads lead in and out of town, there is no convenient nearby harbor where research boats can tie up, and the only airplanes coming in and out of the area are small bush planes. For this reason, doing research in Point Lay depends a lot on scientists working closely with local people. Long-term residents of the area share their knowledge about the seals — but also about weather and ice conditions, navigating through long, shallow Kasegaluk Lagoon, and where the best camping spots are located to stay high and dry in a storm and avoid too-frequent visits by grizzly bears.

When we first began our pilot project to satellite-tag spotted seals in the lagoon in 1992, we went straight to the town elders, Warren and Dorcas Neokok. Warren let us use his boats, guided us to our camping spot, and shared his ideas on catching seals. Dorcas showed us how to stay warm and dry no matter what the weather — and made the best caribou stew we'd ever tasted. We spent long hours talking about when and how spotted seals used Kasegaluk Lagoon, and what haulouts they preferred. Warren and Dorcas told us how they used spotted seals to feed their dogs and clothe themselves during the many years they lived alone at Point Lay.

So just how do you do field work here? We used 16- and 18-foot open aluminum skiffs to boat more than 50 miles up the lagoon to our camping site. Everything we needed — including our fuel and water — had to be packed in the skiffs. When we got there, we set up wall tents that had to sustain 30- to 50-mph winds. The temperature in July and August was sometimes only 30 degrees — a real shock after the 75-degree summer temperatures of Fairbanks. We set 300-foot-long "seal nets" in blustery winds and choppy water — it turned out the seals could see and avoid the net when the weather was good. Our "laboratory" was a blue tarp spread on the sandy beach of a barrier island. We used a small portable generator to power the centrifuge to spin the blood for later lab analyses. What a different field trip than our work in Prince William Sound where we live aboard a self-contained research vessel, complete with hot showers and outlets for our computers.

Today, the school kids in Point Lay can learn from their elders what the seals do in summer, and from space-age technology like satellite tags what they do in winter. ∎

Warren and Dorcas Neokok, Inupiat Eskimo elders at Point Lay, on Alaska's northwestern coast, sit on the beach and watch, along with Sam and Quinn Carroll, as Randy Davis and Geoff Carroll work with a captured spotted seal. (Kathy Frost, ADFG)

Adaptations to Environment

Spotted seals differ from other species in that they regularly haul out on both land and sea ice. The sea ice provides them a clean, mobile platform, remote from most human activities, that they can use to rest between feeding bouts and for other purposes. However, they are not as ice-adapted as ringed seals and cannot maintain holes in unbroken ice, so they are restricted to regions where floes are in motion. Using coastal haulouts during the summer allows them to stay south of the ice, where they have access to the rich food resources of the continental shelf of the Bering and Chukchi seas.

Research on the Species

The basics of the biology of spotted seals were described by Alaskan and Russian researchers examining animals taken by coastal subsistence hunters, by commercial Russian sealing operations

Walrus, also a pinniped, sometimes eat spotted seal pups. Predators other than man include grizzly bears and killer whales. Spotted seals generally live too far south for polar bears to be a threat. (Fred Bruemmer)

and research cruises. Because their population seems to be healthy and there haven't been major conflicts identified, relatively few detailed studies have been done.

In 1992, researchers from ADFG, the North Slope Borough and NMFS began working with people in the village of Point Lay to study spotted seals in Kasegaluk Lagoon. They captured seals in the lagoon, attached satellite-linked tags to 12 of them and tracked their movements. The results were quite remarkable and showed how widely the seals ranged in the waters off western Alaska. Unlike the generally stay-at-home pattern of harbor seals, spotted seals used pretty much all of the continental shelf between Alaska and Russia.

Ribbon Seal

Introduction

The ribbon seal is one of the least known of all the world's seals. Restricted in its distribution to the northern North Pacific, its closest relative is the harp seal of the North Atlantic. Its scientific name, *Phoca fasciata*, means banded seal in Latin, a reference to its striking coloration.

Description —
Size, Coloration, Senses, Vocalizations

Ribbon seals are the most distinctively marked of any of the North Pacific seals. Pups are born in lanugo, and for the first year after the lanugo is shed their coat is silver-gray with a dark blue-black back. Older seals have a dark background with a set of light bands encircling the head, the posterior trunk and each front flipper. In males, the background color is nearly black and the bands almost white. Females have a similar pattern with much less contrast. Adult seals are about 5 feet long and weigh 150 to 250 pounds. They are considerably more slender than other ice-inhabiting seals.

Compared with other seals, the eyes of ribbon seals are quite large. However, they seem to have poor vision in air so this is probably an adaptation for improved eyesight under water. When hauled out on the ice they are easy to approach, but biologists can't say whether this is because they lack good hearing or they simply don't much care about people.

Two kinds of underwater sounds were recorded from ribbon seals in the ice near St. Lawrence Island in spring. One was described as a "puffing" sound, and the other a "downward sweeping" sound. Based on analogy with sounds made by other seals, researchers guessed that the ribbon seal sounds probably were associated with reproductive or territorial behavior.

Distribution, Migration, Population Status

During the spring, ribbon seals are seen on the Bering Sea ice, generally in the same ice-front region where spotted seals are found. They stay close to the ice until it disappears from the Bering Sea in May to June. During summer and fall, ribbon seals are rarely seen hauled out on ice and never on land, and they presumably spend those months living at sea. Their whereabouts are largely unknown, but sightings have been reported near the Pribilof Islands and at the ice edge in the northern Chukchi Sea. One particularly interesting record is of a juvenile male that was caught in a Japanese high-seas salmon gillnet at 51 degrees north latitude, south of the Aleutian Islands, in June 1981. That animal could have come from either the Bering Sea or the Okhotsk Sea breeding populations. In either case, it shows that during summer this species is spread out over a huge area of the North Pacific.

The size of the Bering Sea ribbon seal population has been estimated at about 100,000. In the early and mid-1960s they were heavily hunted by Russian commercial sealers, and those harvests caused a noticeable reduction in the population. Numbers probably

Sexually mature female ribbon seals bear a single pup in early April on open ice floes. This pup is young enough to still have its lanugo coat. (Kathy Frost, ADFG)

recovered after quotas were imposed and hunting pressure was reduced.

Diet, Feeding Habits

During spring when they are in the ice front, ribbon seals eat shrimps, squids and a variety of fishes including arctic cod, saffron cod, pollock, capelin and flatfishes. In places where both species have been sampled, the diets of ribbon seals have been generally similar to spotted seals. Nothing is known about the feeding habits of ribbon seals during summer and fall, which are the seasons when they must feed most intensively.

Breeding, Young

Ribbon seals give birth to pups weighing about 20 pounds in the ice front from March to April. The pup's weight about doubles during a four-

Adult ribbon seals, Phoca fasciata, *have four nearly white bands, one around the neck, another around the rear end of the trunk and one encircling each shoulder. This color pattern gives the species its name. Pups are born covered in lanugo. After six weeks, they shed their white coat, revealing short, sleek hair that is neither banded nor spotted, but has an overall blue-gray cast. (Kathy Frost, ADFG)*

different from other ice-associated seals. While biologists don't completely understand the meaning of these characteristics, it seems likely that they are adaptations to a lifestyle that includes spending many consecutive months at sea. Another unusual characteristic is an air sac that connects to the trachea and extends over the ribs. When inflated this organ could provide extra buoyancy making it easier for ribbon seals to float or rest in the water.

week nursing period. Unlike spotted seals, adult male ribbon seals do not accompany females during the nursing period, and little is known about their breeding behavior.

Predation, Hunting

The ice-front region used by ribbon seals is south of the range of polar bears. During the pelagic phase of their life they undoubtedly encounter killer whales, and perhaps sharks, but no predation events have been reported.

Their offshore distribution mostly keeps ribbon seals away from coastal Alaska hunters, but a few are taken by Eskimos at villages in the Bering Strait region. From 1961 to 1967 the average harvest by the Soviet Union was 13,000 ribbon seals per year. The quota was reduced to 3,000 in 1969. Russia no longer has any significant commercial harvest.

Adaptations to Environment

With their long necks, large eyes and slender bodies, ribbon seals look quite

Research on the species

Most of what researchers know about ribbon seal biology comes from studies done by Soviet scientists as part of the commercial hunt, and from Alaska scientists working from research ships. This relatively thorough knowledge of what these seals do from March to June is in marked contrast to the near-complete lack of information about them at other times of year. New tools, such as satellite-linked tags, are now available and could be applied to ribbon seals to begin to fill this void.

Bearded Seal

Introduction

Bearded seals (*Erignathus barbatus*) are widely distributed throughout ice-covered seas of the Arctic. Two subspecies have been suggested, one eastern and one western, but differences are slight and maybe not significant enough to merit subspecies status. Their common name in the Yupik Eskimo language, *mukluk*, refers to the fact that bearded seal hide has traditionally been used to make soles for boots.

Description —
Size, Coloration, Senses, Vocalizations

Adult bearded seals are a uniform gray or brown color, sometimes with a reddish tinge on the face and front flippers. They are large, powerful animals. Adults are 6 to 8 feet long and weigh as much as 900 pounds, with females slightly larger than males. Their heads look small in proportion to their long, thick body.

There is no specific information on their sensory abilities. After many years of watching bearded seals, researcher John Burns concluded that their sight

Flora Green prepares oogruk, or bearded seal, meat strips and intestines at an Inupiat Eskimo subsistence camp along Kotzebue Sound near the Tukrok River, Cape Krusenstern National Monument. Eskimos also use bearded seal skin for umiak covers and boots called mukluks, *the Yupik Eskimo term for bearded seals. (Fred Hirschmann)*

and hearing are good and their sense of smell is fair. During the spring, bearded seals make fantastic songs that are

Pacific bearded seals are the largest of Alaska's true seals, averaging 475 pounds in summer to 750 pounds in winter. (Fred Bruemmer)

probably associated with breeding behavior. These long, complex warbles are repeated over and over. They can sometimes be heard above the water, although using the Eskimo technique of putting a paddle in the water with the handle at the paddler's ear makes the songs much clearer. We have had

the pleasure of being below the water-line inside large ships and hearing the serenade of bearded seals through the hull. It is certain that males sing, and females may also.

Distribution, Migration, Population Status
Bearded seals are found in ice-covered

regions of the Arctic, mostly over relatively shallow continental shelves. In the winter, bearded seals occur in the ice-front habitat used by spotted and ribbon seals, and also farther north in the pack ice wherever the ice is in motion and there is some open water. They are ice-associated throughout the year, and therefore move north and south as the ice retreats in the summer and advances in the winter. According to coastal residents, some weaned pups do not move northward; they instead spend their first summer and fall feeding in freshwater estuaries along the Bering and Chukchi coasts.

The population size of bearded seals has never been accurately estimated for the Bering-Chukchi seas, or anywhere else for that matter. They are obviously a common animal, and there is no indication that their numbers have changed in recent years.

Diet, Feeding Habits

The diet of bearded seals is much different from that of all other northern seals. While they eat some of the same fishes as do other seals (such as pollock, saffron cod and arctic cod), the bulk of the bearded seal diet is made up of bottom-dwelling invertebrates. Their diet varies by region, but generally consists mostly of shrimps, crabs, clams, octopus and snails. They seem adept at handling these prey, as only the soft parts of snails and clams are eaten. More surprisingly, when we examined the

stomach contents of Bering Sea bearded seals, we often found them filled with the egg-bearing belly flaps from female Tanner crabs. Somehow the bearded seals were able to nip off the part with the caviar without eating the rest of the crab.

Breeding, Young

Bearded seal pups are born on the ice from March to April, but unlike other ice-associated species they are not born with a white, lanugo coat. Instead, pups have a coat of dark, gray-brown wavy hair with lighter coloration on the face. They weigh about 75 pounds at birth and 180 pounds when they are weaned two weeks later. Nothing is known about the details of bearded seal breeding behavior, but their complex songs suggest that they may be territorial.

Predation, Hunting

Bearded seals live in polar bear country, and pups especially may be killed and eaten by bears. During summer, young may be eaten by killer whales. Young bearded seals, as well as young spotted and ringed seals, have been found in the stomachs of walrus.

Bearded seals have been a critical resource for coastal Native peoples for thousands of years. In addition to meat and blubber for food and fuel, their durable hides have been used to make boats, clothing, hunting lines and other items. While times have changed, bearded seals are still a highly sought

Bearded seals have a relatively small head, square front flippers and long whiskers. Their genus name, Erignathus, *is Greek and refers to the deep jaw, while the species name,* barbatus, *is Latin, referring to the whiskers, or "beard." (Kathy Frost, ADFG)*

subsistence resource for Natives living along the coast of western Alaska.

Commercial hunting of bearded seals by the Soviet Union has followed a pattern similar to that for other ice seals.

Solitary except for mother-pup pairs, bearded seals feed in water shallow enough to allow them access to benthic foods such as shrimp, crab, clams, worms, octopus and bottomfish. (Kathy Frost, ADFG)

Annual harvests were several thousand animals in the 1960s, dropping to only 1,000 to 2,000 per year after that, and to virtually zero at present.

Adaptations to Environment

Several traits of bearded seals seem to be adaptations to the threat of polar bear predation. They typically lie with their nose close to the edge of the ice, and if they sense something disturbing, they launch instantly into the water. Their pups are precocious and can swim shortly after birth. This, and their relatively short nursing period, may help to reduce exposure of pups to predation.

The feeding style of bearded seals allows them to exploit a wide range of the food types that occur on the broad, shallow and rich Bering-Chukchi continental shelf. By feeding on benthic invertebrates, they compete less for food with other seal species. Their diet, however, overlaps more with that of walrus, which occur in the same regions and also feed extensively on things such as clams and snails.

Research on the species

The basic biology of bearded seals was described by Alaskan and Russian scientists studying samples from commercial and subsistence harvests and observing animals from ships. Almost no research has been done on bearded seals in the past 15 years, and modern tools have not been used to study the details of their biology.

Ringed Seal

Introduction

The ringed seal (*Phoca hispida*) is the most arctic of all seals, occurring both nearshore and offshore throughout ice-covered northern seas. Several subspecies have been suggested, but their validity and the relationships among them are unclear. The subspecies off Alaska (*Phoca hispida hispida*) is widely distributed and plays a pivotal role in arctic ecosystems.

Description —
Size, Coloration, Senses, Vocalizations

The common name ringed seal describes the adult color pattern—prominent gray-white rings on a dark gray back. The belly is usually silver with few dark spots. Ringed seals are the smallest of the true seals, with adults only 3.5 to 4.5 feet long and weighing 100 to 200 pounds. Their overall appearance is short and round. Size varies quite a lot, with seals off Alaska much smaller than those in eastern Canada.

Ringed seals are very alert when out of the water, and seem to have good eyesight and hearing. They make several types of underwater vocalizations that have been described as "high- and low-pitched barks, yelps and chirps." Since vocalizations are heard at all times of the year, they probably aren't associated with breeding behavior and may aid communication and social organization.

Distribution, Mgration, Population Status

Ringed seals occur throughout the arctic basin. During winter, the highest densities of adult seals occur on the shorefast ice, which provides the most stable platform for pupping. In summer, they occur in the drifting ice and open-water areas. Off western Alaska where the seasonal ice disappears from the Bering Sea and most of the Chukchi Sea during summer, researchers think that ringed seals move northward to follow the ice. In regions like the Beaufort Sea where the ice moves a relatively short distance offshore during

The smallest of Alaska's ice-associated seals, ringed seals have a short, round, gray body with light rings around black spots on their back and sides. (Fred Bruemmer)

summer, the seals are probably much less migratory.

Ringed seals are quite abundant, and given the huge area they occupy, their worldwide population is certainly in the millions. Researchers have never surveyed their entire habitat off Alaska so they don't know how many ringed seals inhabit the Bering, Chukchi and Beaufort seas. Some population monitoring has been done, flying aerial surveys along transects over the ice when seals haul out to bask and molt in June. From

that work, scientists have learned that seal densities vary by location, ice type and year. Over the long term, it is likely that the ringed seal population off Alaska is fairly stable and healthy.

Diet, Feeding Habits

Ringed seals feed on a variety of small crustaceans (euphausiids, amphipods and shrimps) and fishes. They are much more dependent on zooplankton, especially euphausiids, than any other northern seal. When feeding on

FACING PAGE: Ringed seals occur in polar bear territory, and are a favorite meal of Ursus maritimus. *(Scott S. Schliebe, USFWS)*

RIGHT: Ringed seal pups, born with a protective white lanugo coat, begin life in a snow cave that the female digs. While living in these lairs, pups dig many small "pup tunnels," and the lair may expand to include 10 or more chambers and measure 40 feet or more in length. (Lloyd Lowry, ADFG)

zooplankton they are competing for food with other important species like bowhead whales. Their cheek teeth are distinctly multicusped, and look very similar to those of crabeater seals that specialize in eating Antarctic euphausiids. Overall, arctic cod, which have a similar distribution to ringed seals, are probably their most important food. Ringed seals seem to hunt their prey near the bottom, in midwater and along the undersurface of the ice.

Breeding, Young

Ringed seals are unique in that their pups are born in lairs under the snow. The subnivean (under snow) lairs are excavated in snowdrifts above breathing holes that the seals maintain through the ice. The seals dig these holes with the claws on their front flippers. Pups weigh about 10 pounds when they are born in March to April. They are nursed in the lairs for five to seven weeks during which time they double or triple their weight. Their lanugo coat is molted shortly after weaning.

Details of mating are not known, but males are thought to be territorial and may defend areas that contain one or more females in breeding condition. During the breeding season adult male seals have a strong odor similar to gasoline, and they are given a special Eskimo name, *tiggak*.

Predation, Hunting

Throughout the Arctic, ringed seals are of particular importance to three predators: humans, polar bears and arctic foxes. In the high Arctic they are the most dependable, year-round natural resource, and people have used them for food, fuel, clothing and other materials for thousands of years. Ringed seals, especially their blubber, provide the most important food of polar bears, which have devised a number of strategies for catching them. Researchers have estimated that each bear will kill about one ringed seal a

Seal Dogs

By Kathy Frost

Ringed seals live under the solid shorefast ice along the coast in winter. When they are not in the water swimming and feeding, they haul out in small lairs on top of the ice but under the snow where they are invisible to humans. For this reason, they are hard to find and study.

Polar bears and arctic foxes can find these "invisible seals" by using their noses instead of their eyes. They smell seals through the snow. Ringed seal biologists took their cue from these arctic predators, and now use canine research assistants to help them find and study ringed seals in their natural winter habitat. These seal dogs (most often Labrador retrievers) learn to scent seals under the snow and then lead the biologist to the correct spot. It is possible to map the number, types and locations of seal structures in an area with the help of the dogs.

It adds a whole new aspect to field research when the "chief scientist" is a dog. The biologist must make sure the dogs are fed properly, get enough rest, stay warm in the severe cold and have adequate foot protection if the ice and snow are sharp or abrasive. And it also helps to have a tennis ball or a Frisbee handy as a reward for a job well done! ■

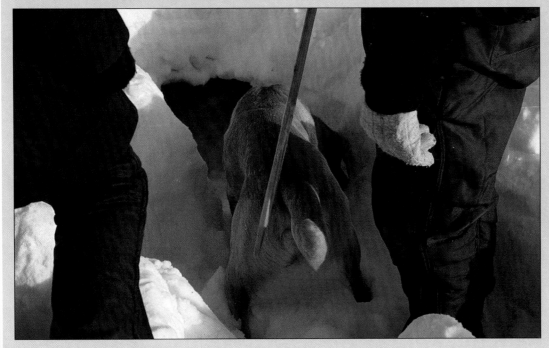

Clyde, trained to aid biologists with research, enters a ringed seal lair. (Kathy Frost, ADFG)

week. Arctic foxes also feast on ringed seals, both the remains of polar bear kills and seal pups that they catch themselves in lairs. Other occasional predators include killer whales, walruses, wolverines, wolves and Greenland sharks.

Adaptations to Environment

Ringed seals are very specialized for inhabiting ice-covered arctic seas. The strong claws on their front flippers are used to maintain breathing holes through ice as much as 6 feet thick, which allows them to occupy the landfast ice region where there are no other holes or cracks. Subnivean lairs provide seals with protection from weather and predators, but this has probably limited the body size of ringed seals since snow accumulations in most areas are not deep. Because they share the sea ice with polar bears, the continuous threat of bear predation has shaped ringed seal behavior. Seals never stray far from a hole or crack into which they can rapidly escape. When lying on the ice, they lift their head every 30 seconds or so and scan their surroundings for bears.

Research on the species

Because of their ecological importance and their unique habitat, ringed seals have been the subject of quite a number of studies. Oil development has expanded from the Prudhoe Bay region northward into nearshore waters where seals live. That has spurred research to monitor population status and to investigate how seals respond to human activities such as island construction and seismic profiling. Dogs, like bears and foxes, can locate ringed seal lairs by smell. Researchers have used trained dogs to locate, describe and map lairs. Seals have been caught in lairs and instruments have been attached to them to study their under-ice diving and navigation. Ringed seals are quite docile and survive well in captivity, so they have

Breathing holes allow ringed seals to remain far from shore in areas of stable pack ice. They maintain the holes with their unusually strong, clawed front flippers, and when hauled out on the ice, keep their heads pointed toward the hole for swift escape from predators. (Kathy Frost, ADFG)

been used as subjects in a variety of laboratory experiments.

Conservation Issues
Health and Diseases

For the most part, seals living off Alaska's coasts seem to be robust and healthy. All seals harbor a variety of parasites in their organs including the stomach, intestines, heart and liver. The parasites are a normal part of the ecosystem, and pass back and forth between the seals and other fish and invertebrate hosts.

Researchers have collected blood from many seals and have done tests for evidence of diseases. Such "serological surveys" don't tell if there is a problem with disease, but only indicate whether or not animals have been exposed to a particular bacteria or virus. Alaska seals show exposure to herpesvirus, distemper virus, caliciviruses, brucellosis, toxoplasmosis and *Chlamydia*. Interestingly, only one ringed seal tested positive for

influenza, and all other species tested were negative.

It's hard to evaluate the significance of disease for the future of Alaska seals. Brucellosis, herpesvirus and *Chlamydia* affect reproduction in other species of mammals, and could cause lower than normal productivity in seal populations. In other parts of the world epidemics caused by distemper virus and influenza have caused major seal die-offs, but biologists have no evidence that this has occurred in Alaska.

Contaminants

Contamination is widespread in the world's atmosphere and oceans. Some of these compounds are left from previous decades of misuse, some are transported long distances from other nations, and others are generated locally in Alaska from things like pulp mills, mining and oil and gas developments. Since seals are predators feeding high on the food chain, they accumulate contaminants in their bodies. The list of possible contaminants is long, including heavy metals (cadmium, mercury, lead, arsenic, etc.), organochlorines (PCBs, DDT, dioxins,

A male northern elephant seal vocalizes, his droopy snout helping the sound resonate. Killed historically for their blubber's high oil content, northern elephant seal populations plunged. Hunting ended in the 1890s, but individuals were not sighted in Alaska waters again until the mid-1960s. (Frank S. Balthis)

ADFG biologist Kathy Frost searches for clues to ringed seal activity hidden under the snow. (Lloyd Lowry, ADFG)

chlordane, etc.) and radionuclides. Organochlorines tend to accumulate in blubber while heavy metals gravitate toward organs such as the liver and kidney. Levels of heavy metals and organochlorines that have been found in Alaska seals are relatively low compared to other areas and may not be of much concern. However, an active area of research deals with the possibility that even low levels of some compounds may impact animal health through suppression of the immune system or endocrine disruption. Another reason to be concerned about contaminants is the fact that seals serve as food for coastal Alaskans. But there is no reason to think that eating seals would pose any serious threat to human health.

Another class of environmental contaminant is called polycyclic aromatic hydrocarbons — oil. Oil is a natural compound, and marine mammals have enzyme systems that allow them to break down and excrete oil so that it doesn't accumulate in their bodies. However, in extreme cases such as the *Exxon Valdez* oil spill, seals that contact highly toxic components of oil (such as toluene and benzene) can suffer nerve damage and die. Impacts on harbor seals were well-documented during the *Exxon Valdez* spill, but it is hard to guess what would happen to seals if a major spill happened in an ice-covered region.

Coastal and Offshore Development

In general, seals seem to tolerate a moderate amount of human activity in their habitats. But they don't exactly like the company of people and if approached too closely, they will flee their haulouts for the security of the water. Apparently harmless activities such as recreational boating and tourism may cause repetitive disturbances that could make seals abandon areas they would otherwise like to use. It's pretty certain that major developments such as ports, harbors, factories, etc. will displace seals if they are built near seal haulout sites. Such factors would be most likely to affect harbor seals and spotted seals that use traditional terrestrial haulouts. But even seals that use offshore ice could be affected by things such as shipping lanes and oil exploration and development.

Hunting

In the past, all species of seals have been commercially hunted. Many years ago bounties were paid on seals in an effort to reduce harbor seal predation on salmon. Harbor seals, especially pups, were harvested at some large haulouts for their fur. The Soviet Union used large multipurpose ships to catch thousands of spotted, ribbon, bearded and ringed seals in the Bering and Chukchi seas. Commercial harvesting of seals in Alaska was outlawed with passage of the Marine Mammal Protection Act in 1972, and since the breakup of the Soviet Union, commercial harvesting by Russia has virtually stopped.

Eskimos, Indians and Aleuts living along the coast of Alaska are permitted to hunt seals for subsistence and to make handicrafts. Subsistence harvests are not large but are important to individual hunters, their families and local economies. Overall, current harvests are probably quite a bit lower than they were in the past. Reasons for that include the reduced use of dog teams that used to be fed seals, a prohibition on the sales of seal skins (unless made into a handicraft), and changes in village lifestyles. Provided that populations are not being impacted by other factors, there is no reason to think that Alaska Native hunting is a threat to seal populations. The Alaska Native Harbor Seal Commission has signed a co-management agreement with the federal government creating a formal partnership to ensure conservation of Alaska's harbor seals.

Fisheries Conflicts

Seals eat seafood, including a number of species that are fished commercially. Harbor seals and spotted seals especially depend on commercially important fishes like walleye pollock, herring and salmon. Ribbon seals may also, but it's hard to say because biologists don't know much about them during the open-water season.

You Can Tell a Seal by Its Spots

By Penny Rennick

Biologists have been working on techniques to identify individual harbor seals, just as they have learned to distinguish individual humpback whales and orcas. Relying on a computer model developed by Lex Hiby of Cambridge, England, Bob Small and Kelly Hastings of ADFG are spearheading a research program to identify individual harbor seals on Tugidak Island southwest of Kodiak.

Small's and Hastings' research depends on the assumption that the pattern of an individual seal's coat remains constant for life. To confirm this, they have worked with aquariums around the country to collect photos of known individuals. The next step usually would call for a person to visually categorize the photos based on shading and pattern, following the practice used in humpback whale and orca identification.

The photos would be catalogued, and when a new photo came in, it would be compared with existing records to identify the animal.

Small was uncomfortable with this approach; he preferred to remove the human element and have the computer assign values to each photo. That's when he heard of Lex Hiby's work with grey seals in England. Hiby had created a three-dimensional computer model resembling a wire grid of a grey seal's head. For harbor seals, a section of the belly rather than the head was a more appropriate area for individual recognition. Hiby designed a grid using a section of the seal's belly. The grid can be adjusted to account for the seal's posture in different photos and can be manipulated to reproduce a two-dimensional patch of the seal's coat. A computer can then subdivide that patch into thousands of cells, and quantify each cell for pattern and shading. Photos of individual harbor seals can be matched with the grid, each patch can be computer-analyzed and thus Small and Hastings can identify individual seals, enabling them to estimate population size, and survival and reproductive rates. ◼

Researchers have developed a computer program to help identify individual harbor seals by specific color patterns on a seal's stomach. (Frank S. Balthis)

A harbor seal is equipped with a satellite tagging device that feeds information about dive depths and times, as well as location of the seal, back to biologists. (Roy Corral)

Bearded seals eat some Tanner crabs but probably not enough to be of concern, and ringed seals pretty much avoid commercially important species. The issues of whether or not seals affect fish stocks and whether fisheries affect seal nutrition are complicated and largely unresolved.

Seals that eat commercially important fishes must feed in areas where commercial fisheries operate. As a result, they are sometimes caught and killed in fishing gear. Observer programs show that a few are caught each year in groundfish trawls and salmon gillnets, but the numbers are too low to have a serious impact on their populations.

Climate Change

Perhaps the greatest concern regarding the future of Alaska's seals is that climate change and/or global warming could impact their habitats. Of most obvious concern is the sea ice. Since several species are adapted to using sea ice for hauling out, pupping, breeding and molting, changes in sea ice characteristics could have major impacts. For example, changes in sea ice that forms in the Bering Sea from winter to spring could have a drastic effect on spotted seals and ribbon seals. The nature of the ice available to them would change (it could be thinner, floes could be smaller, it could have more or less snow), there would be less of it (less room to spread out, more interactions with walruses, less access to preferred feeding areas), and it could melt more quickly in the spring (less time to complete important functions like nursing pups and molting). Parallel changes could occur in the characteristics of shorefast ice, affecting its suitability as breeding habitat for ringed seals. Warming of ocean waters could impact important seal prey, such as herring and arctic cod, and could change the distribution and activity patterns of their predators, such as killer whales and polar bears.

Alaska's seal species face many changes, but they are likely to remain useful and engaging members of the state's marine mammal menagerie. Human understanding of seal habitats will continue to play a part in the lives of these intriguing animals. ■

Seal Bounties and Predator Control

By Penny Rennick

At the beginning of the 21st century, federal and state biologists were working to restore plummeting populations of Steller sea lions and were concerned about serious declines in harbor seal populations. This wasn't always the case, however. Earlier in the 20th century, harbor seals, referred to then as hair seals, were the target of territorial government bounties and predator control programs because they preyed on salmon that were the focus of commercial fisheries.

The 1949 Territorial Legislature authorized a $6 bounty for each hair seal killed in territorial waters from Dixon Entrance south of Ketchikan to Demarcation Point on the arctic coast near the Canadian border. The Legislature appropriated an initial $100,000 to cover bounty payments, an amount that quickly proved insufficient as seal scalps kept arriving at the office of the Territorial Treasurer, in charge of paying bounties, long after funds were gone. The 1951 Legislature had to appropriate an additional $200,000 to cover these claims.

Territorial records showed that by far the majority of hair seal scalps came from northern and western coastal regions of Alaska, "where there [were] no important

Harbor seals counter predators with good hearing and sight, both in and out of the water. (John Hyde)

salmon fisheries and where this animal is an article of food and commerce among the natives."

Though evidence did exist that hair seals preyed on salmon, especially in the Stikine, Copper, and to a lesser extent, in the Taku river deltas, records of hair seal predation on salmon in other areas were problematical. Thus the 1951 Legislature lowered the bounty to $3, and limited the bounty region to those areas with major salmon fisheries and a small section of Seward Peninsula coastal waters. An additional $50,000 was appropriated to fund seal, sea lion and fish predator programs.

The U.S. Fish and Wildlife Service was also undertaking predator control about this time, so officials agreed that federal programs would focus on sea lions and territorial programs on seals. For the Territory of Alaska, this meant primarily the Stikine and Copper river deltas.

Geography and biology influenced how these programs would be carried out. Stikine harbor seals seemed to come and go with the various fish runs, arriving in spring with the smelt and returning in June and throughout the summer with the red and silver salmon runs. The Territory hired two rifleman at $500 per month to shoot seals during a four-and-one-half-month period; they reported a kill of 946 seals for the 1951 season. The same pair were hired the following year, when they reported 768 seals killed.

On the Copper River Delta, harbor seal populations were more concentrated because the animals congregated on river bars. When disturbed, the seals slid into the shallow waters of various channels. Thus territorial agents decided that bombs would make the most efficient weapons. These bombs, made from 10 to 30 sticks of dynamite, could also kill salmon and other animals, so bombing raids were made when they would have the least impact on salmon and other species. Pilots were sent aloft to spot seal herds. Once the herds were located, skiffs with 25-horsepower motors carrying a bombing crew raced down the channels; crews would light bombs with a blow-

One method the government used for culling predators was to bomb areas where harbor seals rested. Hauled out on ice or sand and gravel bars, then taking refuge in the river channels when sensing danger, harbor seals were easy targets. (Robin Brandt)

torch and throw them overboard among the seals. Injured animals were killed with a shotgun when the skiffs made a return run through the channel. Alaska Department of Fisheries (ADF) records indicated that 500 seals were killed in this manner in six days in 1951.

As this technique was perfected and bomb size increased to 50 or more sticks of dynamite, kill numbers rose. Nearly 6,800 seals were destroyed during six bombing expeditions in the Copper River Delta in 1951.

This control program, with some modifications, continued for several years. From 1951 to 1955, bombs killed more than 22,000 harbor seals on the Copper River Delta. Although ADF officers hoped to gain information on harbor seal feeding habits, most of the dead seals sank and their stomachs could not be analyzed for food content. Biologists also wanted to study the effect culling animals would have on the remaining population. At least for harbor seals, the culling did not seem to deter animals in adjoining areas from entering the control area.

From official government programs to kill marine mammals 50 years ago, to million-dollar efforts to restore their populations early in the 21st century, it would seem the study of marine mammals is a complex and ever-changing puzzle. ■

Northern Fur Seals

By Tom Loughlin

EDITOR'S NOTE: *Tom Loughlin is leader of the Alaska Ecosystem Program at the National Marine Mammal Laboratory (NMML), part of the National Marine Fisheries Service (NMFS). His background includes an undergraduate degree in biology, a Masters degree in harbor seal ecology and a Ph.D. from UCLA on sea otter behavior and ecology in California. He has worked for the NMFS as a marine biologist since 1977, and since 1981 has concentrated his research on Alaska issues. The Alaska Ecosystem Program focuses on Steller sea lions and northern fur seals.*

Introduction

The first mention of northern fur seals in scientific literature was Aug. 10, 1741, by German physician/theologian Georg Wilhelm Steller, who recorded in his diary his observations of a "sea ape" while serving as naturalist on Vitus Bering's 1741-42 voyage to Alaska. Steller first noted the fur seal while at sea, about 200 miles from the Shumagin Islands, off the south coast of the Alaska Peninsula. He wrote that the sea ape had "a head like a dog, the ears pointed and erect. On the lower and upper lips on the sides long hairs like a beard, eyes large." He more fully profiled the species on May 28, 1742, while marooned on Bering Island in the Commander Islands, west of the Aleutians, where he measured, dissected and described the outside and inside of a large male.

Description and Habitat

"The ears pointed and erect" as Steller noted, is a characteristic of the family of pinnipeds termed the Otariidae, or "eared seals." The otariids include the fur seals and sea lions and are characterized as having obvious external ears, large front flippers for propelling them through the water, and rear flippers that are pulled up under them when standing on land. Northern fur seals (*Callorhinus ursinus*) occur only in the North Pacific and associated seas. *Callorhinus* is Greek for beautiful (kalos) nose (rhinos), and *ursinus* for bearlike.

The northern fur seal shows extreme sexual dimorphism, meaning size differences between the sexes, with males being two to three times larger than females. Northern fur seal males weigh 400 to 600 pounds and are up to 6.5 feet long; females weigh 65 to 110 pounds and are just over 4 feet long. Newborn pups weigh 10 to 12 pounds, and are about 2 feet long. Adults older than 5 years have long, white vibrissae (whiskers) while juveniles have black ones. The fur seal's waterproof underfur, which numbers more than 350,000 hairs per square inch, is brown, dense and covered by guard hairs that in males vary from black to reddish, with a mane that is often a different color; females are typically brown to gray. This luxurious fur was the focus of an extensive fur trade for almost 200 years.

The largest breeding rookeries for the species occur on the Pribilof Islands in

FACING PAGE: *A northern fur seal waves its huge hind flipper to cool itself. Through a system of blood vessels in the flipper close to the skin, the animal dissipates heat from its body by cooling the appendage. This species is the only marine mammal that can also pant like a dog. (Robin Brandt)*

Thousands of fur seal pups roll and wiggle around rookeries in the Pribilof Islands each summer. After returning from feeding, mothers find their own pup in the crowd by emitting a specific call. Several pups may respond, but the mother is able to recognize her own pup's call and smell. (John Hyde)

the Bering Sea. Fur seals go there to breed and rear their pups, spending the least amount of time possible on land. Males begin arriving two to four weeks ahead of the females to establish and defend territories at sites where females traditionally give birth. Only males holding territories have access to females for reproduction. Females begin arriving on the rookeries from late June to late July and often outnumber territorial males by a ratio of 25-to-1. Females typically give birth to a single pup. Bogoslof Island in the Aleutian Islands is the only other fur seal rookery in Alaska and has grown substantially in the past two decades with over 5,000 pups born there every year.

Female fur seals mature at 3 to 5 years, and most of them between 8 and 13 are pregnant each year. Scientists found one tagged female that was still reproducing at age 25. Males become sexually mature at 5 or 6, but do not usually begin defending a territory until they are much larger and socially mature enough to breed at 9 or 10. Males typically do not survive longer than 17 years.

Senses

Fur seals rely mostly on their senses of smell and hearing; little research has been done yet on their eyesight. Fur seals use smell to locate and identify rookery and haulout sites, females and pups develop recognition at birth through smell and vocalization and both sexes recognize intruders and predators on land by smell. The animals acquire space, reproductive sites and mates through smell, movement patterns and ritualized vocalizations.

A typical fur seal rookery presents a cacophony of noise; animals of both sexes and all ages vocalize for recognition or threat. Both males and females preface movement with vocal displays. Northern fur seals have a unique set of vocalizations related to territorial maintenance and reproduction. Males, when approaching females, make a "wicker" sound that is pulsed like that of a dog barking; after touching noses the male then makes a woofing sound or low roar. Females in estrous vocalize similarly to the bleat of a lamb, although the call is almost inaudible over ambient noise; some females also wicker like the male during pre-copulatory behavior. During territorial acquisition and maintenance, males trumpet a roar toward antagonists.

Migration

Fur seal migration is quite impressive; this species migrates south to California

BELOW: *A rare albino fur seal pup plays with a normal black one. Steller sea lions sometimes kill and eat northern fur seal pups.* (Douglas W. Veltre)

RIGHT: *Able to rotate their hind flippers forward, northern fur seals can "walk" up hillsides away from the beach. Several are hauled out here near rookeries on St. George Island in the Pribilofs. (Alissa Crandall)*

during fall and winter to escape the cold and feed offshore in California and Oregon waters. Typically, fur seals of all ages and both sexes leave the Pribilof Islands in October and November, but some individuals may remain through December. Females and some young males migrate as far south as southern California and are found pursuing prey along the continental shelf; they remain at sea until they return to the Pribilof Islands or other breeding sites in spring and summer. Pup migration is less well known, but scientists think they fan out during their southerly migration, go through the numerous passes in the Aleutian Islands and spend the first two years of their lives throughout the North Pacific, moving between it and the Bering Sea with changing seasons. They commonly do not return to land until their second year. Most adult males winter on both sides of the North Pacific, along the south edge of the Aleutian Islands, in the Gulf of Alaska, or even off the Kuril Islands of eastern Russia.

Eating Habits

The depth to which fur seals dive determines what prey they consume. While feeding, females exhibit two diving patterns: deep diving and shallow diving. The deep-diving pattern appears to be associated with feeding throughout the day over the continental shelf in water less than 660 feet deep. Dives more than 330 feet deep are common and often approach the bottom. On deep dives fur seals typically consume schooling fishes on the continental shelf, such as juvenile pollock, herring and sand lance. Shallow diving is generally restricted to nighttime hours and probably occurs mostly over deep water. These dives typically are about 130 to 300 feet deep, and are thought to follow the movement of the deep-scattering layer, a layer in the ocean that contains organisms ranging from zooplankton to shrimp to small fishes that migrate vertically depending on the intensity of light. On shallow dives, fur seals are most likely to consume squid and deep-sea smelts.

Female northern fur seals from the Pribilof Islands typically depart on feeding trips in late afternoon to early morning and stay at sea three to seven days, sometimes swimming more than

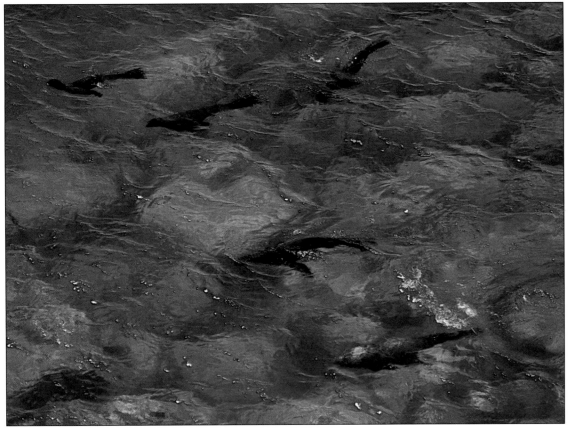

Northern fur seals swim near shore on St. Paul Island. They are primarily fish eaters, consuming about 100 different species. (Loren Taft)

A male fur seal vocalizes to females and a pup. Throughout the breeding season, adult males defending territory inflict wounds on other males. Pups sometimes get squashed by big males in the rookeries. (Roy Corral)

460 miles round-trip. Females swim about 3 to 4 mph while going out, searching for prey and feeding; they travel about 5 to 7 mph on return when they are full of food and heading back to nurse their pup. During this time their pups are left alone on the rookery to fend for themselves. Upon return, the female and pup find each other through vocalizations and smell.

Predation

The effects of predation on the decline and recovery of fur seals are unknown, but probably have not had a major impact on the stock. Killer whales have been observed to attack fur seals near Robben Island in Russia, but no information is available for the Pribilof Islands. Steller sea lions kill weaned fur seal pups close to shore on St. George Island, but generally at rates too low to be significant. The abundance of sea lions has declined, and their predation on young fur seals on St. George has also declined since the late 1970s.

Dr. Terry Spraker, veterinarian pathologist from Colorado State University, has conducted studies on St. Paul Island for the past 13 years to determine the cause of mortality of fur

seal pups and adults. His findings from more than 2,200 pups examined showed that emaciation was the most common cause of death, with trauma (caused by being crushed or bitten by adults) next most common. Emaciation occurred when mother and pup were unable to locate each other and the pup died from insufficient food or dehydration. Adult mortality was caused most often by infected bite wounds.

Role in Alaska's History

The history of the fur seal harvest is a history of Alaska and has been chronicled in numerous publications, one of the best being Alton Y. Roppel's *Management of northern fur seals on the Pribilof Islands, Alaska, 1786-1981* (1984). As mentioned earlier, Steller first sighted and described fur seals in 1741-42. His description of fur seals and sea otters precipitated Russian exploration and exploitation of sea otters in the Commander Islands, Aleutian Islands and other areas of Alaska and the west coast of North America. Exploration and search for more sea otters and the fur

FACING PAGE: *A platform near a rookery on St. Paul Island in the Pribilofs offers visitors a clear view of northern fur seals without disturbing the animals. (Alissa Crandall)*

BELOW: *Arctic fox kits peek out from their den as a fur seal bull enters their territory. (Alissa Crandall)*

seal breeding islands led to discovery of the Pribilof Islands by Gerassim Pribylov, who reached St. George Island in June 1786 and St. Paul in 1786 or 1787. The islands were uninhabited when discovered, but the Russians, spurred by a booming fur trade, imported Aleut Natives from Unalaska Island in the eastern Aleutians to harvest the fur seals, sea otters and arctic blue foxes found in abundance on the Pribilofs. The Natives rotated working every three to four years on the fur seal harvest, with some Aleuts eventually relocating permanently to the Pribilofs. Sea otters were quickly eliminated from

the islands, and fur seals of all ages, but mostly pups, became the focus of the harvest.

From 1786 to 1828 the Russians, with Aleut labor, killed an average of 100,000 northern fur seals per year, primarily pups. Not until 1822 were bulls protected and restrictions placed on the number of pups that could be killed. From 1835 to 1839 an average of 70,000 seals were harvested annually. In 1847 the harvest of females was stopped. During the last 10 years of Russian occupation, from 1857 to 1867, 30,000 to 35,000 fur seals were killed annually.

Then, during the first two years under U.S. control, the fur seal harvest operated without regulations. Approximately 240,000 were taken in 1868 alone. Meanwhile, many fur seals were also killed at sea in pelagic (open ocean) sealing. At the peak of pelagic sealing (1891-1900), more than 42,000 fur seals, mostly lactating females, were killed annually in the Bering Sea. In addition, pelagic sealing was removing a large but unknown number of fur seals from waters off British Columbia. Because the takes were greatly reducing the fur seal stock, Great Britain (for Canada), Japan, Russia and the United States ratified

Northern fur seals have 36 sharply pointed teeth, many of which interlock to hold prey firmly. The upper canines of adult males are about 1 1/4 inches long. (Tom Walker)

the Treaty for the Preservation and Protection of Fur Seals and Sea Otters in 1911. The treaty prohibited pelagic sealing and required a reduction in the number of seals killed on land.

From 1912 to about 1941, Pribilof Island fur seal numbers grew at 8 percent per year under a harvest that ranged from 15,850 in 1923 to 95,000 in 1941. No commercial harvest took place in 1942 because of World War II. The take from 1943 to 1955 averaged about 70,000 per year. From 1956 to 1968, a total of about 300,000 female fur seals

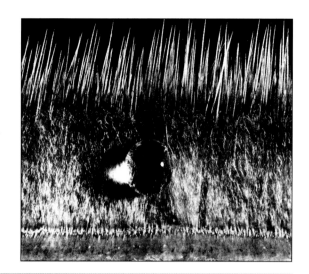

The water-repellent underfur of fur seals effectively prevents the animals from becoming wet. Magnification shown is four times actual size. (From The Northern Fur Seal, *USFWS, 1970)*

were killed on the Pribilof Islands. From then on, up to 1984 when the commercial harvest ended, 30,000 to 96,000 juvenile males were harvested annually.

In 1957, the signatories of the 1911 Treaty ratified a new agreement, the Interim Convention on the Conservation of North Pacific Fur Seals,

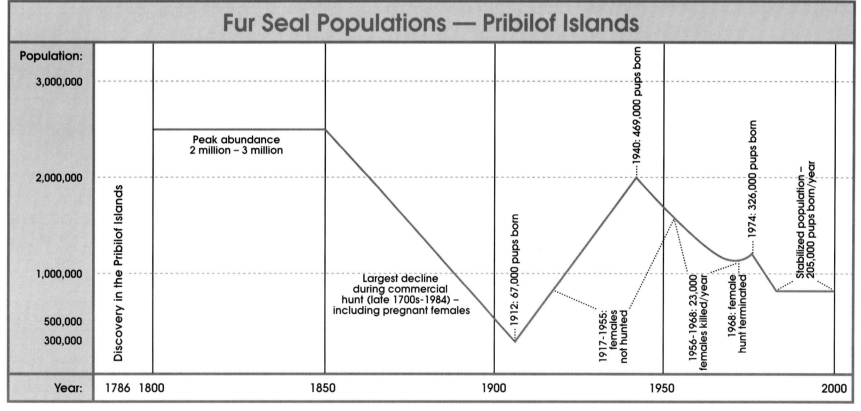

Fur Seal Populations — Pribilof Islands

Population:

- 3,000,000
- 2,000,000
- 1,000,000
- 500,000
- 300,000

Peak abundance 2 million – 3 million

Discovery in the Pribilof Islands

Largest decline during commercial hunt (late 1700s-1984) – including pregnant females

1912: 67,000 pups born

1917-1955: females not hunted

1940: 469,000 pups born

1956-1968: 23,000 females killed/year

1968: female hunt terminated

1974: 326,000 pups born

Stabilized population – 205,000 pups born/year

Year: 1786 1800   1850   1900   1950   2000

for the conservation, research and harvest of this species. In 1973 a moratorium on the commercial take was established at St. George Island, while the harvest on St. Paul continued. Representatives of the United States thought it necessary to establish a research control area on St. George and placed a moratorium on the harvest of fur seals there because of the failure of the Pribilof Islands' population to respond as anticipated to changes in the management scheme started in 1956. A

1998 book by NMML biologist Roger Gentry titled *Behavior And Ecology Of The Northern Fur Seal* details 19 years of research conducted on St. George in response to the closure of commercial harvesting there. On Oct. 14, 1984, the 1957 Interim Convention expired when the United States declined to sign an extension: the commercial harvest on St. Paul Island was terminated and management guidelines reverted to the Marine Mammal Protection Act that allows for a subsistence round-up of

ABOVE, LEFT: *An agile fur seal climbs a barrier to the viewing platform on St. Paul Island. Though less graceful on land than in water, they are powerful animals that should be approached with caution and only if necessary.* (Barbara Willard)

ABOVE: *This northern fur seal exhibits the species' furled pinnae, or ears, and its typical stance on land with front flippers turned out at right angles from the body and bent at the wrists.* (Robin Brandt)

juvenile male fur seals, typically found grouped together at haulout sites adjacent to the breeding rookeries. Once the animals are herded together, those of a certain size (indicating age) are killed. Presently, local Aleut Natives kill about 2,500 subadult male fur seals per year for subsistence use.

Conclusion

One of the most fascinating bits of research conducted on fur seals has been that associated with their behavior at sea and the development of devices that can be attached to them to measure foraging ecology. Dr. Gerald Kooyman and associates at Scripps Institution of Oceanography developed time-depth-recorders that could be attached to a northern fur seal's back. When recovered from the animal, the instruments provided information on the time and depth of dives and allowed speculation on actual foraging ecology and location. With improved technology, the instruments were linked with Argos satellites that pinpointed location during a foraging bout. (Argos was a mythological Greek shepherd with a thousand eyes; even when he slept, he had 50 eyes open to watch his flock.) These instruments help the scientific community gain a broader under-

A biologist crawls carefully along a walkway set up on St. Paul Island for the safe study and observation of northern fur seals. (John Hyde)

Northern fur seals exhibit extreme sexual dimorphism. Mature males can weigh four or five times that of a female. Large bulls vie for reproductive access to females at this noisy rookery. (Roy Corral)

standing of fur seals and of other species with which these animals share the sea.

Further study of northern fur seals and their complex environment will help prevent huge declines similar to those in the late 1800s due to overhunting. Alaska's wildlife is as varied as its ecosystems, and the health of northern fur seal populations contributes to the state's diversity. ■

What Do Fur Seals and Sea Lions Eat?

By Susan Beeman

Steller sea lions' favorite meal is pollock, but they also like herring. Sea lions are opportunistic feeders and eat a variety of creatures including Pacific cod, mackerel, octopus, squid, flatfishes, sculpins and Pacific salmon when seasonally available. Northern fur seals' diet includes sand lance, capelin, squid, deep-sea smelts and herring. Fur seals and sea lions are near the top of the food chain and compete with other marine mammals for the same prey. Weaving this intricate food web even further, Steller sea lions sometimes kill and eat ringed, harbor, spotted and bearded seals and northern fur seal pups. ∎

LEFT: *Walleye pollock, the dominant groundfish species in the Bering Sea, are a favorite meal of both Steller sea lions and northern fur seals. Pollock are usually listed as the world's most abundant fish, but biologists think one factor in declining Steller sea lion populations may be the inability of juvenile sea lions to get enough pollock of a certain size to eat. (Daryl Lee)*

ABOVE: *A Steller sea lion eats a flatfish it has captured and brought to the surface. (John Hyde)*

Steller Sea Lions

By Tom Loughlin

EDITOR'S NOTE: *One of the questions Tom Loughlin and other biologists of the Alaska Ecosystem Program are trying to answer is why Steller sea lion populations continue to decline. The group focuses on ecology, population dynamics, diet and behavior of this species; Tom is particularly interested in the evolutionary ecology of pinnipeds and how they merge life on land with marine life.*

Introduction

The largest member of the Otariidae family of pinnipeds is the sea lion, so named for its resemblance to the terrestrial lion of Africa and Asia. Two species of sea lion exist in the North Pacific: the Steller sea lion and the California sea lion. Long, coarse hair covers the neck and shoulders of mature male Steller sea lions giving them the appearance of having manes. While the California sea lion is rarely seen in Alaska, the Steller sea lion can be found throughout the North Pacific, from California, to Alaska, to Russia and Japan. Despite its wide range, Steller sea lion numbers have declined steadily since the 1970s, and in 1990, the species was listed as threatened under the U.S. Endangered Species Act (ESA).

There were reportedly more than 300,000 Steller sea lions in the world in the late 1970s. It was then that I had the opportunity to assist Clifford Fiscus, a well-known marine mammal biologist, on his last field study before his retirement from government service. Cliff, Ancel Johnson (also a well-known and now-retired sea otter and fur seal biologist from Alaska), David Rugh of the NMML and I surveyed the Aleutian Islands by boat and mapped sea lion rookeries and haulout sites. We found numerous sea lions throughout the island chain and considered the stock to be healthy and robust. However, another group of biologists from our laboratory noted a decline in sea lion numbers a few years earlier in the eastern Aleutian Islands. Since then, the Alaska sea lion population has plummeted to a small fraction of earlier levels.

Description and Habitat

The Steller sea lion is named after Georg Wilhelm Steller. He recorded descriptions of sea lions and fur seals Vitus Bering's crew encountered during the expedition's travels.

Steller sea lion males can be as large as a Kodiak grizzly bear, at about 2,000 pounds and nearly 11 feet long. Females average 550 pounds and are approximately 10.5 feet long. Adult males, although not much longer than females, weigh over twice as much as the average adult female. Pups, at birth, weigh 35 to 50 pounds, are about 3 feet long and are quite docile.

In the sea lion, the fur of both sexes is light buff to reddish brown and is darker (to black) on the chest and abdomen; pups are a deep chocolate brown at birth, then molt to a lighter brown after about 6 months. The fur is coarse and sparse, and thus was not a preferred item in the commercial fur trade of the

FACING PAGE: *A male Steller sea lion looks over pups in a rookery on the White Sisters Islands west of Chichagof Island in Southeast. Females leave their pups periodically to feed at sea. (John Hyde)*

Steller sea lion males can weigh more than a ton. The species is the largest of Alaska's pinnipeds. (James L. Davis)

19th and 20th centuries. They were, and still are, harvested for food by Alaska Natives. Historically, sea lions were used for a variety of purposes: the intestines for making waterproof shirts, throat linings for straps, skin of the flippers for shoe soles, whiskers for decorating caps and hats and hides for covering baidars or skin boats. The fats were saved for use in oil lamps and in cooking.

Steller sea lions live in coastal waters of the North Pacific and have breeding rookeries throughout the region. They are not known to migrate, but they do disperse widely during the non-breeding season. Scientists from the NMML,

Endangered Species Act of 1973

A major tool for the protection of threatened and endangered species, the Endangered Species Act provides for conservation of ecosystems on which wildlife and plants depend. In particular, the act authorizes the designation of species as threatened or endangered; prohibits unsanctioned killing, capturing and transporting of endangered species; sets up a procedure for acquiring habitat important to endangered species; authorizes grants and cooperative agreements for states that have programs to protect endangered species and provides civil and criminal penalties for violations. The act requires federal agencies to refrain from jeopardizing any listed species. Species are listed as "threatened" when they are likely to become endangered and "endangered" when they are likely to become extinct. The Steller sea lion was listed as threatened in 1990; seven years later the western stock of this species was designated "endangered." ■

ADFG and Russia have marked pups in the Kuril Islands that have later been sighted near Yokohama, Japan, more than 220 miles away and in China's Yellow Sea more than 465 miles away. Pups that were marked near Kodiak, Alaska, have been sighted near Vancouver, British Columbia. Generally, animals up to about 4 years of age tend to disperse farther than adults. As

individuals approach breeding age, they usually stay in the vicinity of the breeding islands, and, as a general rule, Steller sea lions return to their island of birth to breed as adults.

Feeding Habits, Diet and Senses

Female Steller sea lions typically feed within 10 miles of their rookery during the breeding season but may go as far as 335 miles or more later in the year. Pups travel less distance while with their mother but may range hundreds of miles from the rookery once weaned. Females usually dive to about 165 feet or less during the breeding season, but often dive deeper, as much as 1,100 feet, later in the year. Pups dive to shallower depths, rarely going below 115 feet. Dives for adult females usually last less than six minutes but may last as long as 11 minutes.

That Steller sea lions interact with commercial fisheries is no surprise since they consume many species targeted by fisheries. Prior to passage of the Marine Mammal Protection Act (MMPA) in 1972, scientists obtained food habits information by examination of stomach contents. In today's conservation-oriented society, killing animals to obtain such data is not acceptable, so food habits information is gathered through analysis of scats (feces) collected at rookery and haulout sites, and in some cases examination of fatty acids and stable isotopes of nitrogen and carbon. By combining information from these sources, biologists have determined the principal prey of Steller sea lions is walleye pollock.

Steller sea lions also eat Pacific cod, Atka mackerel, octopus, squid, herring, flatfishes and sculpins. At specific times of the year sea lions may eat other prey when plentiful (e.g., Pacific salmon). During the breeding season, female sea lions with pups generally feed at night; territorial males do not eat while on territory. Feeding occurs during all hours of the day once the breeding season ends. During this time pups are left alone on the rookery to fend for themselves.

Sea lions are surprisingly agile on land. With large front flippers and strong hind limbs propelling them forward, they can climb rocks and ledges and haul out far above the sea. A sea lion rotates its hind flippers forward under its body when "walking," while swinging its heavy head and neck from side to side for momentum. Underwater, they can swim up to 34 mph in bursts of speed, sometimes "porpoising," or leaping out of the water, during play.

Territorial male sea lion sounds are usually low frequency vocalizations that indicate threats toward other males, courting of females, or are comfort signals. Females vocalize less, at a higher frequency than males. Pups have a bleating cry like sheep, and their voice deepens with age. Adults also vocalize under water, emitting sounds similar to their on-land sounds — barks, clicks, whinnies, moans, growls, squeaks, roars and belches. Female sea lions let out a call to their pup upon returning from feeding in the water. This vocalization, along with the sense of smell and vision at closer range, enables mothers and pups to find each other in crowded rookeries.

Reproduction and Life Cycle

Steller sea lion males establish territories in early May on sites traditionally

Marine Mammal Protection Act of 1972

This act requires the federal government to conserve marine mammals. The Department of Interior is responsible for management of sea otter, walrus, polar bear, dugong and manatee. The Department of Commerce manages cetaceans and pinnipeds, except walrus. MMPA creates a moratorium on taking and importing marine mammals and products made from marine mammals. Exceptions to the moratorium allow Eskimos, Aleuts and Indians to kill marine mammals for subsistence or the crafting of authentic Native articles. The law also allows the Secretaries of Interior and Commerce to issue permits for the taking of marine mammals for public display or scientific research. Later amendments authorized permits for the "incidental" take of marine mammals by commercial fishermen, and under certain other conditions. ■

used by females for giving birth. Pups are born from late May to early July, with most of the births taking place by mid-June. Usually one pup is born; twins are rare. Most females breed again within seven to 10 days of giving birth. Females may nurse their pups from four months up to two years, but pups are generally weaned just prior to the next breeding season.

Pups are capable of swimming within hours of birth, but most remain on shore for at least a month. Mortality among pups is high; perhaps half die in their first year from malnutrition, drowning and predation.

A lone Steller sea lion hauls out on a marker buoy at the south end of Lone Island, in Prince William Sound. (Alissa Crandall)

Birth of a Sea Lion

Photos by James L. Davis

While assisting ADFG biologists, photographer Jim Davis captured this birth sequence on Fish Island, easternmost of the Wooded Islands southeast of Montague Island, in the Gulf of Alaska.

Steller sea lion pups are born with their eyes open and are able to crawl, and if necessary swim, a few minutes after birth.

Adult females bond only with their own pup and are aggressive toward others, sometimes lifting stray pups off the ground with their teeth and tossing them.

After giving birth, the mother remains with her pup at the rookery for one to two weeks, then goes to sea to feed. Several hours later, she returns to suckle her pup.

This pattern continues until the pup is about 1 month old and follows its mother on her feeding trips.

Females are ready to breed about 12 days after they give birth, though egg implantation is delayed for three and one-half months. The peak mating season in Alaska is late June to early July. ■

Scientists have speculated that the rate of killer whale consumption of Steller sea lions has increased during recent decades and may contribute to observed declines in sea lion abundance in Alaska. Studies at the University of British Columbia to assess the possible impact of killer whales has found that killer whale predation did not cause the sea lion decline, but because the populations are so low in some areas, killer whale predation may now be a contributing factor. This study estimated that approximately 18 percent of sea lions that die annually in western Alaska may be eaten by killer whales.

The role of disease in the life of these pinnipeds is not well understood, but is likely not a major factor. Blood taken from Steller sea lions in Alaska contained antibodies to two types of bacteria (*Leptospira* and *Chlamydia*), one marine calicivirus (San Miguel Sea Lion Virus), and seal herpesvirus (SeHV), all of which could produce reproductive failure or death. The incidence of these pathogens in the population was low and not considered significant enough to cause observed declines.

An Endangered Species

The Steller sea lion was originally listed as "threatened" throughout its range because there were no data to determine the existence of separate stocks. Recent studies of mitochondrial

DNA from Steller sea lions throughout the range suggests that at least two stocks exist, an eastern stock (California through Southeast Alaska) and a western stock (Prince William Sound and areas west). The genetic information, coupled with information on movement patterns, trends in population dynamics and low immigration rates suggested two stocks that should be managed differently. The listing of the western stock was changed from threatened to endangered in 1997.

The magnitude of the decline in such a short time is startling. Historically, the Gulf of Alaska and Aleutian Islands contained the largest fraction (74 percent in 1977) of the world population of Steller sea lions, but by 1989 it dropped to 56 percent. The rookery at Walrus Island (one of the

Sea lions tend to swim in large groups when feeding on non-schooling prey. Their diet conforms to seasonal and regional availability of species. (John Hyde)

smaller Pribilof Islands) once was the birthplace of more than 2,800 pups annually; in 1991 only 50 pups were counted. Once Marmot Island near Kodiak was the largest Steller sea lion rookery in the world. In 1979, 6,741 pups were born there; only 804 pups were observed in 1994. Similar declines have occurred in both adult and pup counts in most of Alaska and Russia.

Scientists studying this phenomenon thought that perhaps Alaska sea lions had redistributed to other parts of the range, but that was not the case. From 1955 to 1968 the Steller sea lion population in the Kuril Islands, Russia, was stable at about 15,000-20,000 individuals, but it has declined steadily since that time to 5,000 counted in 1989. Presently the Russian population

may be stable but reliable counts have not been obtained for the entire Russian region. The Kuril Islands support the largest group of Steller sea lions in Russia including the primary rookeries where 98 percent of pupping in Russia takes place.

Reasons for the decline in sea lion numbers are unknown but may be linked to reduced availability of prey caused indirectly from environmental changes or commercial fishing activities, or both. Results of many years of research on Alaska sea lions by now-retired ADFG biologist Don Calkins and colleagues has provided important clues to the possible cause of the decline in numbers. His work pointed toward a nutritional problem, likely caused by reduced prey availability, that decreases the fitness of young animals. Both severe environmental disturbances and commercial fishing, resulting in changes in the abundance or availability of prey, have been implicated in declines in pinniped abundance. Other factors, such as disease, contamination, predation by killer whales and subsistence harvest by Alaska Natives, have been mentioned as possible causes but

A Steller sea lion pup squawks for its mother on Forrester Island in Southeast. Females usually have a higher frequency vocalization than do males, even when young. Highly vocal pinnipeds such as sea lions tend to be more social than their quieter cousins. (John Hyde)

Two male sea lions fight for territory on Lowrie Island in the Forrester Island Wilderness of Southeast. Dominant males, usually 9 or older, establish breeding territories on rookeries in early May, then mate with sexually mature females from May through July. (John Hyde)

are not now deemed the principal cause for observed declines.

Changes in the environment indirectly influence sea lions principally by affecting their prey. If environmental changes altered the abundance or availability of a necessary prey, pinniped survival and productivity could be reduced. These types of responses have been observed in some seals and sea lions in California and South America during 1982-83 and 1997-98 as a result of strong El Niño (warm water) events, and in South Africa and Namibia in 1993 and 1994, perhaps because of changes in prey distribution. Evidence that major shifts have occurred in the abundance of fish and shellfish in the Bering Sea during the past several decades is well-documented; factors responsible for these changes, however, are not. There has been a general warming trend in the Bering and Okhotsk seas during the past three decades, and shifts in temperature and wind patterns may have affected fish and shellfish population trends. Information, however, linking environmental variability to specific changes in fish recruitment (survival of young animals to

reproducing age) is largely absent. Since 1932, northeast Pacific Ocean environmental variability has been characterized by alternating warm and cool eras of six- to 12-years duration. The decline in Steller sea lions continued unabated during both types of eras. The relationship, if any, between the sea lion decline and environmental changes remains to be seen.

Steller sea lions are killed incidentally to commercial fisheries. In the United States, the current level is considered to be low (less than 50 animals per year) and is not a likely cause of observed declines. An unknown number are shot each year in fisheries and for illegal sport, but this number too is assumed to be low at present. Approximately 500 are killed each year by Alaska Natives for subsistence purposes. Sea lions are also killed in Japan, but the actual number is unknown; a harvest by the Japanese has been estimated based on interviews with local authorities. During 1991-93 an average of 91 sea lions were killed per year; a high of 247 sea lions were killed annually during 1981-85. This harvest comes from sea lions inhabiting the coast of Asia with breeding rookeries on islands and along coastal areas of Russia, the Kuril Islands, the Okhotsk Sea, the Commander Islands and the Kamchatka Peninsula. Steller sea lions are considered by some in Japan to conflict with commercial fish harvests and are therefore subject to a directed kill to reduce or eliminate damage to gear and depredation on fish stocks. In this harvest, the government commissions hunters to shoot sea lions within Japanese territorial waters. Some of the carcasses are recovered and some samples are made available for scientific studies. Some of the meat is recovered and processed into a canned product that is then sold, primarily as a novelty to tourists. The fact that sea lions marked in the Kuril Islands have been sighted in Japanese waters suggests that a significant portion of the sea lions that are killed incidental to fisheries in Japan may be from the Kuril Islands stock.

Seining for Sea Lions?

Photos by John Hyde

These Steller sea lions popped up inside the loop of a commercial fishing boat's seine in Stephens Passage in Southeast Alaska. Since fishermen and sea lions compete for many of the same resources, they often come into conflict. Steller sea lions are on the Endangered Species List and even though poachers do occasionally shoot them, it is illegal.

The fishermen on the *Leading Lady* tried to scare the sea lions off by splashing the water's surface with a plunger, but that didn't even get a second look. Patiently, they let the sea lions have their fill of pink and chum salmon trapped inside the net. The animals jumped safely over the corkline and swam away.

Researchers don't yet have a definitive answer to the reason for the Steller sea lion population decline, but implementing government programs that restrict the amount of resources commercial fishing fleets catch is one option marine mammal managers have to help solve the situation. ■

Management

Federal and state governments, the commercial fishing industry and the environmental community have developed a remarkably good working relationship in addressing the Steller sea lion population decline. Opinions differ as to the cause of the decline and how to best conserve sea lions, but these differences have been manifested in healthy debate working toward a common goal. But what else can be done? Scientists are not sure what additional management measures need to be implemented. The government does not want to impose regulations that might needlessly stifle the fishing industry, yet the government is required to protect and conserve this species. There seems to be little doubt that sea lions and commercial fishing efforts concentrate on the same prey, yet it is not fair to imply that the fishing fleet is responsible for the decline given the available data. However, the fleet bears the brunt of the management regime since the government is required to do its best to stop the decline and facilitate recovery; management of the fishing fleet is the parsimonious way to do this. For example, the United States has implemented numerous fishery management schemes to protect Steller sea lions in Alaska trawl fisheries. These include time and area closures that vary during the year depending on the location and fishery involved. Marine mammal management agencies will be challenged in the next several years to identify and mitigate the causes of the decline and to create meaningful protective measures for a declining species without further restricting the nation's fisheries.

In April 1990, the NMFS established a Steller Sea Lion Recovery Team consisting of 11 government and private sector biologists. This team prepared a Steller Sea Lion Recovery Plan that was submitted to NMFS and published in 1992. The Plan summarizes available data on the species and decline and suggests research and management actions needed to facilitate recovery of the species.

Conclusion

Steller sea lions and all other marine mammals generally exhibit low to modest changes in population numbers that fluctuate with the carrying capacity of their habitat. They do not have the ability to recover quickly from large declines in abundance since they breed at most annually and have only one offspring. Large natural declines in numbers are rare and are typically related to a disturbance, such as a disease. Scientists have no record of any marine mammal species that has undergone a natural decline in numbers to levels currently experienced by the Steller sea lion and which later recovered to previous levels. Of course, some species have been driven to very low levels by commercial exploitation, and some of them have recovered while others have not. The declines observed

BELOW: *Sea lions sometimes get caught in fishing nets and drown or, like this one, struggle with a piece of gear that gradually cuts into the flesh around its neck. (Tom Walker)*

RIGHT: *Orcas, or killer whales, are the Steller sea lions' only predator of any consequence, other than humans, in Alaska. (John Hyde)*

in Steller sea lion numbers are not solely a result of a natural fluctuation or a recurring cycle. If they were, then such declines would likely have occurred at other times in the evolutionary history of Steller sea lions, and it is unlikely that the species would have recovered from all of them.

In response to the Steller sea lion being listed under the ESA, the United States designated as critical habitat all Alaska rookeries, major rest sites and nearby waters, and three aquatic areas (Shelikof Strait between Kodiak and the Alaska Peninsula, Bogoslof Island just north of the eastern Aleutians and Seguam Island in the central Aleutians) known to be used by sea lions during certain times of the year. For the endangered western stock of Steller sea lions, that totals about 121,350 square miles, roughly the same size area as one-fifth of Alaska. Scientists hope these measures give Steller sea lions a chance to increase their numbers so that Marmot Island and other rookeries are once again filled with the commotion of a thriving Steller sea lion population. ∎

LEFT: *Pinniped species occasionally meet in common waters, like this walrus and sea lion circling each other off Round Island in Bristol Bay. (Tom Walker)*

BELOW: *Japanese fishermen compete with Steller sea lions for some of the same resources, and sea lions within Japanese waters are subject to a controlled harvest to keep their numbers down. Some of the meat is canned and sold to tourists as a novelty. (Courtesy Bob Juettner, Aleutians East Borough)*

FACING PAGE: *Fish Island off Montague Island in Prince William Sound is home to Steller sea lions throughout the summer. (James L. Davis)*

Sea Otters

By James Bodkin

EDITOR'S NOTE: *Jim Bodkin is a research scientist with the Alaska Biological Science Center in Anchorage. He began his career with sea otters in California in 1980 and has studied them throughout the northern Pacific Ocean. He currently leads the Coastal Ecosystem Research Team whose work has focused on sea otters and nearshore marine communities.*

Introduction

Sea otters have been an important resource for people living along the North Pacific coast for thousands of years. At least two aspects of the sea otters' natural history have linked them with humans: their pelt and their food habits. Sea otter pelts, arguably the finest in the animal kingdom, were fashioned into garments, particularly in northern latitudes, while the presence of sea otters influenced the availability of some marine invertebrates, like snails, clams and abalone, that provided food for coastal people. In addition, sea otters spurred a growing fur trade after Vitus Bering's explorations of the North Pacific in the early 1700s revealed their widespread abundance. This commercial harvest was instrumental in European exploration and settlement of the Pacific Rim and led to the near-extermination of the sea otter, *Enhydra lutris*, in following centuries.

Largely because of their life history and their direct relations with coastal residents, sea otters are a comparatively well-understood marine mammal. During the past few decades, concern for sea otters has broadened to encompass an interest in global resource conservation and restoration, as well as community ecology. This more recent focus on sea otters now extends to humans far removed from marine environments.

Early sea otters evolved about 12 million years ago from Eurasian and African ancestors. They reached the North Pacific by way of two proposed migration paths, one along the Bering Land Bridge between northeastern Asia and northwestern North America and a second from the Atlantic Ocean that entered the Pacific through a channel in the central Americas. Modern sea otters occur only in the North Pacific and have occupied their current range for the past 1 million to 3 million years.

Environment, Food Habits and Movements

Sea otters are the only exclusively marine member of the Mustelidae (otter, weasel, badger and skunk) family, and are capable of spending their entire lives in the ocean. They are closely related to other otter species, such as the river, clawed, giant and smooth otters that occur on all continents and are mostly freshwater forms. One poorly known species, the marine otter (*Lutra felina*) of the west coast of South America, forages exclusively in marine habitat but acts out most other behaviors ashore along rocky coastlines.

Sea otters occupy nearly every coastal marine habitat in the North Pacific, from shallow estuaries to the exposed outer coasts. They are gregarious, and

FACING PAGE: *Sea otters inhabit shallow coastal waters with sandy or rocky bottoms that support crabs, mussels, urchins, clams and fish. (Patrick J. Endres)*

Sea otters haul out on an iceberg in Unakwik Inlet, northern Prince William Sound. When they come ashore, they usually form sex-segregated groups of a few to hundreds of animals. (Alissa Crandall)

often rest in groups numbering from a few to many hundreds. Kelps that form floating canopies are favored resting areas, but sheltered bays or offshore rocky areas that block wind and waves are also used for resting. Individuals may leave the sea to rest on ice floes, sand-bars or intertidal rocks, but no aspect of

a sea otter's life history requires such behavior and some never come ashore.

Although sea otters share adaptations found in other diving mammals such as collapsible lungs and hind feet modified for underwater locomotion, they are unique in that they feed almost entirely on benthic invertebrates such as crabs, clams and snails rather than the fish, squid or zooplankton many marine mammals eat. They also are known to chew open cans they find on the floor of California's Monterey Bay to reach octopus that hide inside. Sea urchins probably rank no. 1 on a list of more

than 100 species of food items sea otters eat. Sea urchins range in maximum size from about that of a baseball to that of a softball.

Sea otters generally forage alone, but feeding individuals may concentrate where prey is most abundant. Although they are capable of diving to more than 325 feet, most feeding takes place in waters less than 150 feet deep. Because sea otters feed primarily on organisms living in, or on, the sea floor, their distribution offshore is limited by their ability to dive to the ocean bottom. And although they can be found far from shore where shallow waters occur, they are most common in waters adjacent to the coastline.

They are relatively sedentary compared to most marine mammals, and most individuals occupy home ranges that might include a few tens of miles of coastline. Juveniles and adult males tend to have slightly larger home ranges. Because of limits in their diving ability, effective barriers to movement exist in the form of deep and wide passages between suitable habitats, such as islands. Because of their limited movements, exchange of genetic material over long distances can require many generations.

Life Cycle and Reproduction

Sea otters mate at all times of the year, and young may be born in any season. In Alaska, most pups, averaging 3 to 5 pounds, are born in late spring. A newborn pup is particularly vulnerable to predation and starvation, and requires almost constant care. If the mother is in poor condition when her pup is born, she may not be able to provide adequate care without risking her own life. Thus, most pup mortality occurs during the first 60 days after birth. If she is able to bring the pup through this period, the mother will likely raise it to weaning age. However, if she loses her pup at this early stage, she mates soon after and is able to produce another pup within the same year.

Sea otters can live more than 20 years, although the average life span for males is about 10, and 15 for females. A female reaches sexual maturity between ages 2 and 4. She is pregnant for about six months and produces a single pup, an adaptation to aquatic living common among marine mammals but not seen in other otter species. Population growth rates are constrained by the production of a single offspring. On rare occasions, twins are born. The reproductive rate increases with age, until by age 5 about 90 percent of females are giving birth to a pup per year. This annual reproductive

Grooming their thick fur is an important activity for sea otters. Unlike seals, which have a thick layer of blubber to insulate them, sea otters instead have the densest fur of any mammal. Air trapped between long guard hairs and soft underfur buoys them and helps keep their skin dry and warm. (Dan Parrett)

output is maintained throughout adulthood with only a slight decline late in the female's life.

Pups depend on their mother for up to one year, during which the pup develops to near-adult size and acquires the skills it will need to live on its own. During their first year of life, pups are susceptible to various sources of mortality including hypothermia, predation, starvation and disease that can vary greatly and depend on the environmental conditions in which they

were born. In areas where populations are at or near carrying capacity and food is relatively scarce, survival of pups can be as low as 45 percent, but where sea otter populations have abundant food supplies, the survival of pups can be as high as 85 percent. A second critical period of a pup's life comes at weaning and for several months afterward when the chance of mortality again rises. Survival rates can drop to 20 percent after weaning, although they may be as high as 85 percent under good

conditions. Survival generally increases following the first year of independence, approaching 90 percent for adult males and 95 percent for adult females.

Sea otters are polygynous, with dominant males defending territories where females are present and excluding other males. The sexes are generally segregated, with the best habitat occupied by females and their young; most males, except those holding territories in female areas, concentrate in relatively small areas. The sex ratio at birth is about 1:1, but generally fewer males survive. The male-biased mortality results in a sex ratio among adults that is skewed toward females, which can comprise 70 percent of the population. Thus a reproductive system with more females than males in the population allows for higher population growth than if the sex ratio were equal.

Luxurious Fur: A Special Adaptation

Because water conducts heat more than 25 times faster than air, aquatic mammals, particularly those occurring in high latitudes, require advanced

LEFT: *In Kachemak Bay in lower Cook Inlet, a mother sea otter and her pup float, the pup resting on her stomach. The peak breeding season in Alaska is September through October, and females normally bear one pup in May. The offspring of first-time mothers have a lower survival rate than do the offspring of experienced mothers. (Alissa Crandall)*

BELOW: *Guard hairs and thick underfur, magnified 75 times, from the midback of an adult male sea otter show the density of the species' pelage. The circular areas represent the guard hairs, the squiggly areas the underfur. (Karl Kenyon, USDI)*

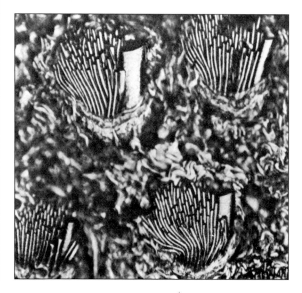

Sea otters bring their food to the surface to eat. A loose pouch of skin on each foreleg is used to carry food, so an otter can gather several pieces during one dive, then bring them all to the surface at once. Typically, a sea otter will use only the pouch on the left for storage, leading researchers to think most sea otters are "right-handed." (Tom Walker)

adaptations to maintain their constant body temperature. The adaptation employed by virtually all other marine mammals is one of a fat or blubber layer that encases the body and provides insulation.

Sea otters lack this blubber layer; instead, they produce the densest fur of all mammals to insulate themselves. This luxurious coat consists of two types of hair: a dense underfur that traps air and coarse guard hair that forms a protective outer layer. The up-to-1-million hairs per square inch of a sea otter's fur are quite capable of keeping the skin and underfur dry, insulating the otter with a layer of air, as opposed to fat.

The quality, or insulating properties, of a mammal's fur in large part depends on the habitat in which the animal lives. Species occupying the coldest habitats are considered to have the highest quality of fur. Humans initially valued mammal fur as a source of insulation. With proper clothing, people could occupy cold arctic habitats. Furs assumed additional value as a symbol of wealth and status, the finest furs having

Sea otters wrap themselves with kelp before sleeping to prevent drifting, though this is not necessary for survival. In places in the Bering Sea, they seem to sleep comfortably without secure kelp beds. (Chlaus Lotscher)

the highest value, both in insulating quality and social status. Thus the value of sea otter fur to both the otter and the human can ultimately be traced back to the biology of the animal.

Sea Otters and Humans:
Indigenous Use

Researchers have little direct knowledge of the interaction between indigenous people of the North Pacific and the sea otter. However, we can draw some inferences from what exists in archaeological remains throughout the Pacific Rim as well as from written history following Bering's explorations.

Two lines of evidence support the premise that early coastal dwellers used

sea otters. First, skeletal remains of these animals are common in coastal middens, the accumulated refuse at sites of human occupation. These middens exist throughout the Pacific Rim and provide insights into coastal people's lives and the resources they used. Second, and even more convincing, is that coastal people, particularly in northern regions of the Pacific, had apparently developed an elaborate and efficient method for hunting sea otters long before acquisition of modern firearms. In particular, the Aleuts had developed a sophisticated hunting strategy prior to 1750. The hunt consisted of a well-coordinated effort that required specialized tools and the skills of many individuals. The Aleuts would take to the sea in small one- or two-man skin kayaks and paddle in formation searching for otter. The hunters likely concentrated on areas favored by sea otters for either resting or feeding. The typical response of sea otters to disturbance is to dive, and they can stay submerged for nearly five minutes, although average dive times are between one and two minutes. Upon locating one or more otters, the hunter in the kayak closest to the animal would raise his paddle to alert the others that an otter had dived. The remaining hunters would then form a broad circle around the location where the otter was last seen and wait for it to surface. This process would be repeated until the otter under pursuit surfaced sufficiently close to a hunter to be struck with a small spear propelled with a sling. A line attached to the spear was used to retrieve the animal; often more than one spear would be required to kill the otter. The development of such sophisticated, cooperative hunting is ample evidence of the importance of sea otters well into human history.

At least one other method was occasionally used to hunt sea otters and required an understanding of the close relationship between a female sea otter and her pup. At birth, a sea otter pup is largely defenseless, incapable of most behaviors other than nursing and floating on the water's surface. The mother is forced to leave the pup on the surface alone because she must still dive to the sea floor to forage. These separations create opportunities for predators, including the bald eagle and humans. The helpless pup is easily captured and handled without its mother and early hunters would entwine the pup with line and hooks. The pup would then become bait to lure the highly protective mother. While retrieving her pup, the female would

A sea otter eats a fish near Whittier in Prince William Sound. Sea otters use their front paws, which have retractable claws, for eating and grooming, but not for swimming. (Alissa Crandall)

become snared in the line and hooks and be subdued by the hunters. The pup depends on its mother for about six months and although pups of all ages can be readily captured without the protection of their mothers, they probably became less susceptible to this hunting technique with age.

Researchers have little knowledge of exactly why early coastal people hunted sea otters, but the hunters' elaborate methods confirm that they did indeed harvest them. We can, however, speculate on at least three potential reasons: one that is associated with management and protection of alternative resources and two that relate to resource acquisition, fur for clothing and as a commodity for trade.

Sea Otters as a Keystone Species

The concept of harvesting sea otters to protect other resources requires an understanding of the complex role this species can play in structuring coastal marine communities. Sea otters provide one of the best examples of the ecological "keystone species" concept. Simply put, a keystone species is one that has a proportionately greater effect on the community in which it exists than might be expected by its abundance.

The best evidence to support the sea otter as a keystone species comes from kelp forest communities of shallow rocky areas along the North Pacific coast. Within these habitats reside several species of sea urchins, marine herbivores that actively graze on algae, including the brown algae that form the often-conspicuous underwater kelp forests that occur along many coastlines. Where sea otters are abundant, they effectively control sea urchin populations by consuming most individuals larger than about 1 inch in diameter. Those larger sea urchins that escape sea otter predation do so by taking refuge in crevices that otters cannot reach. As a result, when sea otters are present, urchins generally do not have much of a grazing effect on algae and consequently kelp forests flourish.

Alternatively, in the absence of sea otters, sea urchin populations increase their numbers and average size. As this happens, the sea urchins exert greater grazing pressure on the kelp forest and can ultimately eliminate the forest and much of the associated animal community. An urchin-dominated community, sometimes called an urchin

Sea Otters as Tool Users
By Susan Beeman

Sea otters are the only mammal, other than primates, to use tools for eating. Most of the invertebrates sea otters eat have hard shells and must be cracked open to get at the meat inside. After bringing crabs or mussels or clams up from the ocean bottom, the sea otter rolls onto its back, and placing on its stomach a flat rock it has held under its arm, bangs the invertebrate on the rock several times to crack it open.

Pups learn from an early age the hammering skills they will use as adults. They begin by making chest-slapping motions at about 5 weeks, and at about 10 weeks, are rubbing pieces of shell together, or diving while holding a rock. By the time they are 5 months old, young sea otters seem adept at either biting into the shells of their prey or using a rock to help crack it open. ■

A sea otter carries a stone, used to help crack open shellfish, under its arm. (Frank S. Balthis)

An excavation of the Korovinski site on Atka Island in the Aleutians reveals thick volcanic ash covering layers of shells in a midden, or refuse pile, left by indigenous peoples. Researchers think that historical coastal Alaska Natives understood the effect sea otters had on local populations of shellfish, especially sea urchins. (Douglas W. Veltre)

barren, is characterized by abundant, large sea urchins, little midwater habitat provided by kelp and the absence of kelp-associated fauna.

Biologists have observed similar effects in other prey species in the absence of sea otter predation. For example, some species of crabs, abalone and mussels can also increase in abundance and average size once sea otters are removed. Those prey populations that flourish in the otters' absence can become more available for other predators, such as humans. While biologists cannot definitively answer whether early coastal people controlled sea otter populations to enhance populations of other invertebrates for their own use, they certainly possessed the knowledge, tools and abilities to do so. The presence of bones and other items these early people discarded in their village middens suggests that they may have done just that.

Excavated middens on Amchitka Island in the central Aleutians reveal distinct layers that apparently represent periods of time in which large sea urchins were abundant, as well as periods when they were rare. Although alternative explanations are possible, this finding coincides with periods of time when otter abundance may have been regulated by human harvest and resulted in distinct changes in the composition of coastal marine communities, as evidenced by the large sizes of sea urchins. A similar pattern can be seen in middens in islands off California, where the remains of shells of large abalone, mussels and urchins are present. The abundance and large size of these invertebrates, which are preferred sea otter prey, is inconsistent with the relative scarcity of large individuals of those same species in marine communities today where sea otters are present.

Although factors other than human harvest, such as starvation, disease or other predators may regulate sea otter populations, the midden remains and the well-developed hunting methods indicate that early coastal residents

Flourishing kelp beds in known sea otter territory may be a sign that the otters are keeping sea urchin populations down. (James Bodkin)

exploited sea otter populations as a tool to enhance desired invertebrate resources that could be used as food. It was in fact the hunting skills of coastal people within the sea otter's range that facilitated the commercial harvest of this species, a prowess that eventually led to the otters' near-extinction.

Sea Otters as a Fur Resource

Vitus Bering's discovery of abundant sea otters in the North Pacific and Bering Sea in the early 1700s spurred a commercial sea otter industry that lasted a century and a half and eventually reduced the number of sea otters from perhaps 300,000 to a few hundred. Initiated by Russians, the hunt began in the western Pacific, the Kuril and Commander Islands of Russia and the far western Aleutian Islands. Spanish, British and American fur hunters eventually joined in. The harvest progressed to the east as sea otters were removed from successive island groups in the Aleutians. Indigenous coastal hunters, primarily Aleuts, were employed, or in some cases enslaved, to conduct the hunt using those hunting methods described above. Eventually the Russians established trading centers at Kodiak and Sitka to handle the furs and other commerce. The primary market for sea otter pelts was Asia, where furs returned about $30 per pelt in the early 19th century. An estimated 500,000 to 900,000 sea otters were killed between 1742, when the commercial harvest began, and 1910, when the unsuccessful final hunt was held.

Despite the obvious value of the resource, there was apparently little effort to manage the harvest in any way that might assure its continuation. In fact, it is unlikely that the hunters knew how to harvest sea otters in a way to ensure the population, although historical records indicate that the Russians did make rudimentary efforts at conservation. A review of the commercial hunt in light of current understanding of a sea otter's life history may help explain how this species could have come so close to extinction.

Using advanced molecular techniques, researchers are able to distinguish genetic differences between populations as close together as Prince William Sound and Kodiak Island. The unique gene frequencies found within and among isolated sea otter populations confirm their limited movement and geographic isolation. Thus the appropriate scale at which the commercial hunt could have been managed would have been over a much smaller area than the entire Pacific Rim. In other words, if the average harvest of 3,000 to 5,000 per year had been distributed in proportion to their overall abundance, rather than removing all otters from successive hunting areas, it is unlikely that the species would have approached extinction nearly a century ago. It is also possible that biologists would not have even been able to detect a decline in the overall abundance of the species during the period of commercial hunting.

Recovery of Sea Otter Populations

By the close of the 19th century it was clear that sea otter populations were too low to support a commercial harvest of any kind. Ironically, not until 1911, one year after the final hunt, did sea otters receive political protection under the

Fur color is one indication of age in sea otters. Adults range from dark brown to blonde; their head and neck lighten with age until they become white in old animals. Sea otters usually live 15 to 20 years. (Frank S. Balthis)

North Pacific Fur Seal Convention. Eleven geographically isolated sea otter populations — mostly in the Aleutians and Southcentral Alaska with a few in Russia and one in California — survived the commercial slaughter and formed the nucleus for recovery of the species.

During this period of low or no sea otter presence, profound changes occurred in marine communities formerly occupied by the otters, changes that provided cash and crops for humans but may have hindered the recovery of sea otters. In addition to increased sea urchin grazing, which reduced kelp biomass, a number of other species of mollusks, echinoderms and crustaceans were spared the effects of sea otter foraging. Over time, these species grew in number and size and attracted the attention of people, who recognized that these species could support a commercial harvest. During the 20th century, commercial fisheries developed for abalone, clams, sea urchins, crabs and spiny lobster. It is worth noting that most of these commercial harvests have also resulted in depletion of populations and fishery closures. In addition, a large number of recreational and subsistence fisheries have also developed in response to the large invertebrates present in the absence of sea otter predation. This modern scenario of increasing invertebrate populations and their use by humans following sea otter reductions may not be too much different from that described in the Aleutians during thousands of years, except in terms of geographic and economic scale.

Conflict has arisen where humans harvesting these invertebrates have met sea otters recolonizing their range. These conflicts have led to increased levels of illegal human kill of sea otters, either in frustration of suffering economic loss or in an effort to prevent that loss. In either case, the interests of people who oppose the recovery of sea otter populations today clash with the dramatically different interests of those concerned with conservation and restoration of natural communities. The latter view sea otters as an integral component of the coastal marine community, valued for

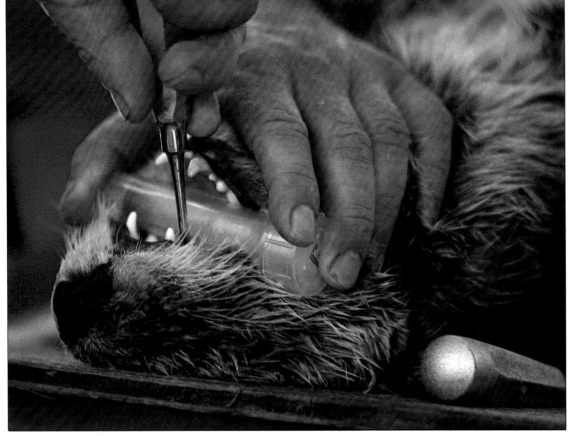

A biologist extracts a tooth from a sea otter during research eight years after the 1989 Exxon Valdez *oil spill, which left thousands of marine animals and birds dead or injured. (Roy Corral)*

Sea otters were hunted, almost to extinction, for their luxurious fur. The commercial harvest of Enhydra lutris *stopped in 1911, and populations now thrive in Alaska. (Tom Walker)*

their presence rather than because of economic gain from their harvest or as an ecological consequence of their absence. Further, this perspective can be and is held by humans that do not reside along the coasts.

Recovery rates of remnant sea otter populations appear to have varied, particularly in the first few decades following protection. The Amchitka Island population grew the fastest, about 13 percent annually. Nearly all other remnant populations had average annual growth rates of 10 percent or less. The California population, numbering a few dozen in 1914, showed the slowest growth. Eighty-five years later, the population only numbers about 1,800. One explanation for the slow growth may be that the populations were so small that even the additional mortality of a few animals could offset the growth potential offered by reproduction in a given year. Arrests and the recovery of pelts prove that some illegal hunting occurred in the early 20th century. The sea otter's social and reproduction systems could have imposed a third limitation. Perhaps otters were so few and so sparsely dispersed, or sex ratios so skewed by the hunt, that reproductive rates were impaired.

Whatever the reasons for the various growth rates, they were adequate to produce healthy and growing populations throughout much of Alaska, central California and Russia by the middle of the 20th century.

Translocations

By the 1960s and 1970s sea otter populations were sufficient to begin translocating animals from Amchitka Island in the Aleutians and Prince William Sound in Southcentral Alaska to

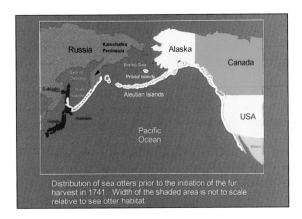
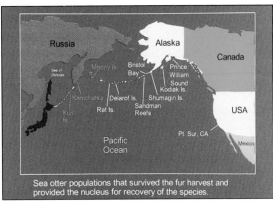
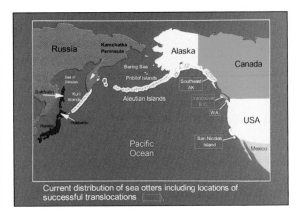

Distribution of sea otters prior to the initiation of the fur harvest in 1741. Width of the shaded area is not to scale relative to sea otter habitat.

Sea otter populations that survived the fur harvest and provided the nucleus for recovery of the species.

Current distribution of sea otters including locations of successful translocations

These maps show sea otter distribution at three stages: before the beginning of commercial hunting, remnant populations after the hunting stopped and current distribution. (Courtesy James Bodkin)

Oregon, Washington, British Columbia, Southeast Alaska and the Pribilof Islands. The goal of these translocations was to re-establish sea otter populations in their former range. These translocations would help the species recover and might also provide animals for a second commercial hunt. Accurate estimates of the current number of animals in each of the translocated populations are not available, but the Southeast Alaska population, founded with an estimated 150 animals in 1969, could exceed 20,000 animals in the year 2000.

The Oregon and Pribilof translocations failed; the Washington and British Columbia efforts succeeded, with current populations numbering in the thousands. Each of the translocated

populations experienced high losses initially, either through mortality or emigration. During the mid-1980s, 142 sea otters were translocated from central California to San Nicolas Island off southern California. In 1999, a count at the island revealed 23 animals, the highest count in more than 10 years. The ultimate fate of this colony remains uncertain, but the lack of population growth demonstrates the high initial rate of loss of translocated otters. Despite more than 50 pups being born since the translocation, there has been no increase in population on San Nicolas, which confirms the existence of decline and a delayed growth phase after initial release.

The sea otter translocations gave biologists an opportunity to study another aspect of population dynamics, the effects of population reductions (or bottlenecks) on genetic diversity. Reduced genetic diversity can impair the ability of a population to recover by limiting reproductive rates or

increasing mortality. Sea otters provide a good case study of the effects of population reductions on genetic diversity and population recovery rates because of the number of isolated remnant colonies and the number of translocations to isolated areas.

We recently used population and genetic data from four remnant and three translocated populations to test for relations between magnitude and duration of population declines and genetic diversity and population growth rates. We found that both the duration and magnitude of the decline correlated positively with genetic diversity, but did not find the expected relation between decreasing genetic diversity and reduced population growth rates. We also found that translocated populations experienced higher population growth rates than did remnant populations, and translocations using two different sources displayed increased genetic diversity. The reasons for differences in growth rates are unclear, but likely are

Caring for "Eyak"

By Pam Tuomi, D.V.M.

EDITOR'S NOTE: *Dr. Pam Tuomi has practiced veterinary medicine for 30 years in Anchorage. She participates in projects with U.S. Fish and Wildlife Service, U.S. Geological Survey, Canadian Wildlife Service and Alaska Department of Fish and Game, working with migratory birds, walrus, seals and sea otters. Her current position as veterinarian for the Alaska SeaLife Center, in Seward, supports the Center's mission of research, rehabilitation and education and provides routine health care for their collection of Steller sea lions, harbor seals, birds, fish and invertebrates.*

This sea otter pup weighed 5 1/2 pounds and was 3 to 4 weeks old when found July 8, 1996, drifting alone in northern Prince William Sound. A severe storm the preceding night had apparently separated the pup from its mother. The U.S. Fish and Wildlife Service, with management responsibility for sea otters in the United States, investigated. Unable to locate any other otters in the area, they brought the pup to the Alaska Wildlife Response Center in Anchorage, where a temporary nursery was set up. In August, the nursery moved to an outdoor site donated by the Alaska Zoo, and the orphan "Eyak" helped visitors learn about his species.

A sea otter pup is totally dependent on maternal care for five to six months. The mother must constantly groom her single pup to keep it meticulously clean and waterproofed. Properly aligned, the dense fur holds an insulating air layer next to the skin. The mother otter floats on her back and holds her pup on her stomach where it sleeps, nurses and stays warm and dry. While she dives for food, she releases the pup to float on the surface. Pups may appear "abandoned" during these dives but should always be observed from a distance. Usually, the mother surfaces to retrieve her pup and start the grooming process over again.

At a nursery, trained volunteers stay with an orphan 24 hours a day to provide a continuous cycle of feeding, swimming practice, grooming and sleeping. Formula is made from pureed clams, squid, half-and-half, electrolyte solutions, vitamins and cod liver oil. The pups are taught to nurse from a baby bottle and require 20 to 25 percent of their body weight each day in food. At 6 weeks, they start to eat small bits of shellfish meat and play with shells. They love to hold and manipulate rattles, balls, teething rings and other baby toys and to sleep on a cool waterbed mattress or in a hammock just above their swimming pool. Young pups must learn to roll over, swim and dive in a shallow saltwater pool and must be thoroughly combed and dried after each swim until old enough to groom themselves. Temperature control is critical, as sea otters can easily become hypothermic when wet or overheat when dry.

Captive-raised sea otter pups become dependent on humans and usually cannot be released into the wild. Lifelong homes must be found for them in one of a handful of zoos and aquariums with adequate facilities. In 1995, the Blijdorp Zoo in Rotterdam, The Netherlands, offered a permanent home to another Alaska orphan, "Chuluugi," the first sea otter to live in Europe. The U.S. Fish and Wildlife Service agreed to send "Eyak" to Blijdorp as a companion for "Chuluugi." On September 10, 1996, "Eyak," his veterinarian and a U.S. Fish and Wildlife Service representative made the long trip on a cargo jet by way of Frankfurt, Germany. Both otters have thrived in Rotterdam ("Eyak" now weighs 68 pounds) and are moving into a spacious new exhibit pool designed to educate visitors about life in polar regions. ∎

Dean Rickerson, a volunteer at Anchorage's Bird Treatment and Learning Center, bathes and dries "Eyak," an orphan sea otter pup picked up by USFWS. Volunteers had to teach the pup how to dive by dropping baby toys to the bottom of his pool.
(Harry M. Walker)

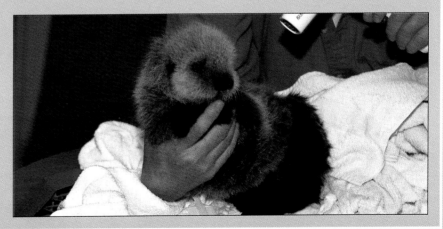

related to site specific differences in survival.

From most perspectives, the overharvest and near-extinction of sea otters should be considered a tragedy. However, from at least one perspective, this situation provided unprecedented opportunity in the study of large mammals. When biologists study captive populations of invertebrates, a larval beetle for example, it is relatively straightforward to manipulate population size and provide controls for those manipulations, allowing scientists to rigorously assign cause and effect (or not) to the experimental manipulation they impose. For both practical and ethical considerations, large carnivores are difficult to experimentally manipulate. In the case of the sea otter, by selecting study areas with and without sea otters, or by selecting areas for study over time as recolonization occurs, biologists have been able to evaluate many aspects of the otter's ecology and natural history. Good examples of the results of this approach are demonstrated in the descriptions of the role of sea otters as keystone predators in coastal marine communities and the effects of sea otter reductions on population genetics and recovery rates.

The Future

Our view of coastal marine communities and the role of sea otters in those communities has been shaped to a large degree by what we observed during the 20th century, when sea otter numbers increased from a few hundred animals distributed over thousands of miles of shoreline to many tens of thousands of sea otters currently

FACING PAGE: *A raft of sea otters floats near Augustine Island, an active volcano in lower Cook Inlet. (Don Cornelius)*

RIGHT: *Sea otters are strong swimmers, and alternately roll onto their stomach and float on their back. (James L. Davis)*

occupying more than half of their historic range. Suitable, unoccupied habitat remains, and it appears likely that sea otter populations will continue to recover. However, as local population densities reach equilibrium with food and space resources, we might expect rather large declines in local populations. Such a phenomenon was recently observed at Bering Island in Russia where the population experienced a large-scale die-off that led to a

population decline from about 5,000 animals to 3,000 in a single year. Nearly 80 percent of the recovered carcasses were male, resulting in a surviving population with an increased proportion of females. Similar phenomena might be expected as recovery continues, particularly at islands where emigration might be limited or in mainland populations where the distance to unoccupied habitat exceeds the dispersal distance

of sea otters. As unoccupied habitat shrinks, it seems unlikely that we will continue to see the high growth rates in populations that we observed in the 20th century.

Sea otter fur spurred Russian hunters to cross the Bering Sea to the Aleutians. A thriving fur trade with the Chinese lasted more than a century. (Roy Corral)

Future decisions regarding management and conservation of sea otter populations at or near equilibrium with their food and space resources may require a perspective quite different from that developed during the past century. Sea otters will likely remain important to humans. As they continue to recover previous habitat, conflicts can be expected where humans and otters compete for valuable invertebrate resources, particularly in Japan, Southeast Alaska, British Columbia, Pacific states of the United States and Mexico. Although we probably have adequate information on the life history of sea otters to conduct a sustainable harvest, social and ethical considerations from a geographical scale that extends well beyond the people and shores of the North Pacific must now be considered. ■

Bibliography

Annual Report, 1950-1955. Alaska Board of Fisheries and Alaska Department of Fisheries. Juneau: Territory of Alaska, 1950-1955.

Bonner, W.N. *The Natural History of Seals.* London: Christopher Helm, 1989.

Burns Sr., John J., ed. *Marine Mammals Species Accounts: Wildlife Technical Bulletin No. 7.* Alaska Department of Fish and Game, 1984.

Caldwell, Francis E. *Land of the Ocean Mists: The Wild Ocean Coast West of Glacier Bay.* Edited by Robert N. DeArmond. Edmonds: Alaska Northwest Publishing Co., 1986.

Gay, Joel. *Commercial Fishing in Alaska,* vol. 24, no. 3. Penny Rennick, ed. Anchorage: Alaska Geographic Society, 1997.

Gentry, Roger. *Behavior And Ecology Of The Northen Fur Seal.* Princeton: Princeton University Press, 1998.

Haley, Delphine, ed. *Marine Mammals of Eastern North Pacific and Arctic Waters.* Second Edition, Revised. Seattle: Pacific Search Press, 1986.

Henning, Robert A., ed. *Islands of the Seals: The Pribilofs,* vol. 9, no. 3. Anchorage: Alaska Geographic Society, 1982.

Lentfer, Jack W., ed. *Selected Marine Mammals of Alaska: Species Accounts with Research and Management Recommendations.* Washington, D.C.: Marine Mammal Commission, 1988.

Love, John A. *Sea Otters.* Golden, Colo.: Fulcrum Publishing, 1992.

Rearden, Jim, ed. *Alaska Mammals,* vol. 8, no. 2. Anchorage: Alaska Geographic Society, 1981.

Rennick, Penny, ed. *Restoring Alaska: Legacy of an Oil Spill,* vol. 26, no. 1. Anchorage: Alaska Geographic Society, 1999.

—. *Mammals of Alaska.* Alaska Geographic Guides series. Anchorage: Alaska Geographic Society, 1996.

—. *The Bering Sea,* vol. 26, no. 3. Anchorage: Alaska Geographic Society, 1999.

Ridgway, S.H. and R.J. Harrison, eds. *Handbook of Marine Mammals. Vol. 2, Seals.* New York: Academic Press, 1981.

Riedman, Marianne. *The Pinnipeds: Seals, Sea Lions, and Walruses.* Berkeley: University of California Press, 1990.

Roppel, Alton Y. *Management of northern fur seals on the Pribilof Islands, Alaska, 1786-1981,* Technical Report NMFS #4. NOAA, 1984.

Scheffer, Victor B. *The Year of the Seal.* Illustrated by Leonard Everett Fisher. New York: Charles Scribner's Sons, 1970.

Senungetuk, Joseph E. *Give or Take A Century.* San Francisco: The Indian Historian Press, 1971.

Wynne, Kate. *Guide to Marine Mammals of Alaska.* Illustrated by Pieter Folkens. Fairbanks: Alaska Sea Grant College Program, University of Alaska Fairbanks, 1992.

Websites
www.state.ak.us/local/akpages/FISH.GAME/ notebook/marine/ (Alaska Department of Fish and Game) ∎

Index

PHOTOGRAPHERS

ALASKA GEOGRAPHIC® Back Issues

The North Slope, Vol. 1, No. 1. Out of print.
One Man's Wilderness, Vol. 1, No. 2. Out of print.
Admiralty...Island in Contention, Vol. 1, No. 3. $19.95.
Fisheries of the North Pacific, Vol. 1, No. 4. Out of print.
Alaska-Yukon Wild Flowers, Vol. 2, No. 1. Out of print.
Richard Harrington's Yukon, Vol. 2, No. 2. Out of print.
Prince William Sound, Vol. 2, No. 3. Out of print.
Yakutat: The Turbulent Crescent, Vol. 2, No. 4. Out of print.
Glacier Bay: Old Ice, New Land, Vol. 3, No. 1. Out of print.
The Land: Eye of the Storm, Vol. 3, No. 2. Out of print.
Richard Harrington's Antarctic, Vol. 3, No. 3. $19.95.
The Silver Years, Vol. 3, No. 4. $19.95.
Alaska's Volcanoes, Vol. 4, No. 1. Out of print.
The Brooks Range, Vol. 4, No. 2. Out of print.
Kodiak: Island of Change, Vol. 4, No. 3. Out of print.
Wilderness Proposals, Vol. 4, No. 4. Out of print.
Cook Inlet Country, Vol. 5, No. 1. Out of print.
Southeast: Alaska's Panhandle, Vol. 5, No. 2. Out of print.
Bristol Bay Basin, Vol. 5, No. 3. Out of print.
Alaska Whales and Whaling, Vol. 5, No. 4. $19.95.
Yukon-Kuskokwim Delta, Vol. 6, No. 1. Out of print.
Aurora Borealis, Vol. 6, No. 2. $19.95.
Alaska's Native People, Vol. 6, No. 3. Limited.
The Stikine River, Vol. 6, No. 4. $9.95.
Alaska's Great Interior, Vol. 7, No. 1. $19.95.
Photographic Geography of Alaska, Vol. 7, No. 2. Out of print.
The Aleutians, Vol. 7, No. 3. Out of print.
Klondike Lost, Vol. 7, No. 4. Out of print.
Wrangell-Saint Elias, Vol. 8, No. 1. Limited.
Alaska Mammals, Vol. 8, No. 2. Out of print.
The Kotzebue Basin, Vol. 8, No. 3. Limited.
Alaska National Interest Lands, Vol. 8, No. 4. $19.95.
Alaska's Glaciers, Vol. 9, No. 1. Revised 1993. $19.95.
Sitka and Its Ocean/Island World, Vol. 9, No. 2. Out of print.
Islands of the Seals: The Pribilofs, Vol. 9, No. 3. $19.95.
Alaska's Oil/Gas & Minerals Industry, Vol. 9, No. 4. $9.95.
Adventure Roads North, Vol. 10, No. 1. $19.95.
Anchorage and the Cook Inlet Basin, Vol. 10, No. 2. $19.95.
Alaska's Salmon Fisheries, Vol. 10, No. 3. $19.95.
Up the Koyukuk, Vol. 10, No. 4. $9.95.
Nome: City of the Golden Beaches, Vol. 11, No. 1. $19.95.
Alaska's Farms and Gardens, Vol. 11, No. 2. $19.95.
Chilkat River Valley, Vol. 11, No. 3. $9.95.
Alaska Steam, Vol. 11, No. 4. $19.95.

Northwest Territories, Vol. 12, No. 1. $9.95.
Alaska's Forest Resources, Vol. 12, No. 2. $9.95.
Alaska Native Arts and Crafts, Vol. 12, No. 3. $24.95.
Our Arctic Year, Vol. 12, No. 4. $19.95.
Where Mountains Meet the Sea, Vol. 13, No. 1. $19.95.
Backcountry Alaska, Vol. 13, No. 2. $19.95.
British Columbia's Coast, Vol. 13, No. 3. $9.95.
Lake Clark/Lake Iliamna, Vol. 13, No. 4. Out of print.
Dogs of the North, Vol. 14, No. 1. $21.95. Limited.
South/Southeast Alaska, Vol. 14, No. 2. Limited.
Alaska's Seward Peninsula, Vol. 14, No. 3. $19.95.
The Upper Yukon Basin, Vol. 14, No. 4. $19.95.
Glacier Bay: Icy Wilderness, Vol. 15, No. 1. Limited.
Dawson City, Vol. 15, No. 2. $19.95.
Denali, Vol. 15, No. 3. $19.95.
The Kuskokwim River, Vol. 15, No. 4. $19.95.
Katmai Country, Vol. 16, No. 1. $19.95.
North Slope Now, Vol. 16, No. 2. $9.95.
The Tanana Basin, Vol. 16, No. 3. $19.95.
The Copper Trail, Vol. 16, No. 4. $19.95.
The Nushagak Basin, Vol. 17, No. 1. $19.95.
Juneau, Vol. 17, No. 2. Limited.
The Middle Yukon River, Vol. 17, No. 3. $19.95.
The Lower Yukon River, Vol. 17, No. 4. $19.95.
Alaska's Weather, Vol. 18, No. 1. $19.95.
Alaska's Volcanoes, Vol. 18, No. 2. $19.95.
Admiralty Island: Fortress of Bears, Vol. 18, No. 3. Out of print.
Unalaska/Dutch Harbor, Vol. 18, No. 4. $19.95. Limited.
Skagway: A Legacy of Gold, Vol. 19, No. 1. $9.95.
Alaska: The Great Land, Vol. 19, No. 2. $9.95.
Kodiak, Vol. 19, No. 3. Out of print.
Alaska's Railroads, Vol. 19, No. 4. $19.95.
Prince William Sound, Vol. 20, No. 1. $19.95.
Southeast Alaska, Vol. 20, No. 2. $19.95.
Arctic National Wildlife Refuge, Vol. 20, No. 3. $19.95.
Alaska's Bears, Vol. 20, No. 4. $19.95.
The Alaska Peninsula, Vol. 21, No. 1. $19.95.
The Kenai Peninsula, Vol. 21, No. 2. $19.95.
People of Alaska, Vol. 21, No. 3. $19.95.
Prehistoric Alaska, Vol. 21, No. 4. $19.95.
Fairbanks, Vol. 22, No. 1. $19.95.
The Aleutian Islands, Vol. 22, No. 2. $19.95.
Rich Earth: Alaska's Mineral Industry, Vol. 22, No. 3. $19.95.
World War II in Alaska, Vol. 22, No. 4. $19.95.

Anchorage, Vol. 23, No. 1. $21.95.
Native Cultures in Alaska, Vol. 23, No. 2. $19.95.
The Brooks Range, Vol. 23, No. 3. $19.95.
Moose, Caribou and Muskox, Vol. 23, No. 4. $19.95.
Alaska's Southern Panhandle, Vol. 24, No. 1. $19.95.
The Golden Gamble, Vol. 24, No. 2. $19.95.
Commercial Fishing in Alaska, Vol. 24, No. 3. $19.95.
Alaska's Magnificent Eagles, Vol. 24, No. 4. $19.95.
Steve McCutcheon's Alaska, Vol. 25, No. 1. $21.95.
Yukon Territory, Vol. 25, No. 2. $21.95.
Climbing Alaska, Vol. 25, No. 3. $21.95.
Frontier Flight, Vol. 25, No. 4. $21.95. Our 100th Issue!
Restoring Alaska: Legacy of an Oil Spill, Vol. 26, No. 1. $21.95.
World Heritage Wilderness, Vol. 26, No. 2. $21.95.
The Bering Sea, Vol. 26, No. 3. $21.95.
Russian America, Vol. 26, No. 4, $21.95
Best of ALASKA GEOGRAPHIC®, Vol. 27, No. 1, $24.95

PRICES AND AVAILABILITY SUBJECT TO CHANGE

Membership in The Alaska Geographic Society includes a subscription to *ALASKA GEOGRAPHIC*®, the Society's colorful, award-winning quarterly.

Contact us for current membership rates or to request a free catalog. *ALASKA GEOGRAPHIC*® back issues listed above are also available. **NOTE:** This list was current in mid- 2000. If more than a year has elapsed since that time, contact us before ordering to check prices and availability of back issues, particularly for books marked "Limited."

When ordering back issues please add $5 for the first book and $2 for each additional book ordered for Priority Mail. Inquire for postage rates to non-U.S. addresses. To order, send check or money order (U.S. funds) or VISA/MasterCard information (including expiration date and your phone number) with list of titles desired to:

ALASKA GEOGRAPHIC®

P.O. Box 93370 • Anchorage, AK 99509-3370
Phone: (907) 562-0164 • Toll free (888) 255-6697
Fax (907) 562-0479 • e-mail: info@akgeo.com

Visit us!
www.akgeo.com

NEXT ISSUE: VOL. 27, NO. 3
Painters of Alaska

To present a different view of the Great Land, we offer a look at Alaska through artists' eyes. Written by Kesler Woodward, a painter himself and the state's foremost author on Alaska art, this text explores painting in the North from early Native artists, through legendary pioneer painters to contemporary stylists. To members fall 2000.